AUTISM: ONE FAMILY'S JOURNEY

Autism: One Family's Journey

1st edition

ISBN: 978-0-6151-6317-8

Cover design by Alana Boldt and Miles Boldt

Acknowledgement

I would like to thank C.W. for his support and also for twenty years of urging me to share my family's journey. I can only wish you the very best fortune in your travels, also.

I would like to acknowledge all of the wonderful people who have supported and protected Shane on his life's path. You know who you are.

For Angie and Glenda, thank you!!! That 'thank you' would also embrace those other entities who bring me smiles on life's journey.

Acknowledgement and heartfelt gratitude also goes to Miles for designing the cover of this book, as well for formatting this book multiple times!

I would offer a special 'thank you' to Elaine for her input into my project.   The personal and professional miles you have logged in your fight for the handicapped can only polish your soul!

L.G., your editing skills are so much better than mine. I thank you for your proofreading, even if it did lead to a hasty revision of the book! (Smile)

I would wish to acknowledge the people who currently and continually struggle with autism. I would like to acknowledge those persons who are no longer with us. Your struggles were during times when help was not available. You received little or no understanding or support. You are not forgotten.

Foreword

It has taken twenty years of urging from a valued friend for me to make the decision to put our life's journey into words, into a book. I want to acknowledge to the world that my son and oh, so many other persons, are absolutely beautiful and gifted people under their cloaks of autism.

I have met many young parents over the past years who have shared their concerns over their child's autism. Sometimes they confide their concerns over their own lives and how they have been affected personally. I understand their fears, their confusion, and their anger. I have been there. I have over three decades of being mother to a handsome son who struggles with severe autism. I share our story in hopes it may be of help to one of these young parents. I would hope knowledge of my mistakes, as well as our successes, might be of benefit to someone just starting their journey.

Almost two decades ago, Shane and I were out for yet another car ride. The day was sunny and beautiful. Because he was so pleasant and happy, I thought it would be rewarding to stop at a small country store to purchase a snack for him. He headed directly for the small deli and gazed in awe at the array of cheeses on display. He became slightly animated as he pointed to several. He was obviously excited and joyous at the sight of the abundance of cheese varieties. A man came up beside me and loudly stated that children 'like that' should not be allowed in public; they should remain at home behind locked doors. I was blindsighted and could not respond. We left (with cheese). The incident did not appear to ruin Shane's day, but I was crushed. The middle aged farmer had the audacity to speak such a cruel remark not only to me, but in my son's presence.

Later in my years of working with developmentally disabled people, I was to hear and witness many other incidents of cruelty and rudeness while we were in public areas. I expect stares and questions from very young children; it is how we learn. I do *not* expect it from adolescents and adults. Rudeness and cruelty are an outward display of ignorance and a lack of respect for life. Perhaps someday all members of society will learn to accept each other.

Even though society has come a long way in its understanding and 'acceptance' of autism, we still have a very long way to go. Each parent will have to take their own journey and come to terms with how their lives will be changed. Even though there is more help available than there was thirty years ago, it can be a painful and isolated journey. I am concerned about the well being of these young parents.

When I meet a young mother for the first time, I let her know that I have, as a mother, survived autism. Some mothers want to know what my son is like as an adult. I hesitate to share Shane's current life portrait because I don't want them to stereotype the progress we've experienced as being gospel, or concrete. Nothing is written in stone. Every entity comes into this existence with his or her own very personal path to walk. Some individuals make great strides of progress in their life. Some do not. Rarely, we read in highly publicized reports that a few individuals have 'come out of' their autistic state completely.

I write this book in an attempt to offer support. While it hasn't been the life I had planned for, it has been a full life. In retrospect, I can honestly say I would not trade what I have been through…for anything.

I would also offer my writing to those souls who spent their entire lives locked within themselves. I apologize that we, as a society, misunderstood you.

For Shane
For your bravery and courage

To Miles
For your support and very presence in my life

Part I
The Journey

It is mid-morning on a late summer day. I look at my son sleeping in his living room recliner. He has grown into a handsome man. His face still bears the almost angelic quality that was prevalent when he was born. Under his baseball cap his hair is thinning and aged scars on his scalp are more visible. He wears the stubble of not having been shaved since yesterday. He is resting peacefully and his breathing is even. I hope he is finding respite from his waking hours.

I wonder what he dreams about. Sometimes he 'talks' in his sleep. His verbalizations are as unintelligible as when he is awake. At other times, he may giggle and smile during his sleeping hours. I wonder what realm he visits during his hours of sleep.

I wonder if he realizes how very much I love him. I wonder what life would have held for him, had his life path had not been effected so deeply by circumstances beyond anyone's control.

The man who had worked as my son's direct care staff overnight said they had a very good night. They went for a car ride and stopped in at a store to do some light shopping. Shane had eaten well and was calm.

I could breathe a bit easier. Unless I am summoned during the night, I do not know what to expect when I first see him in the morning. Life is akin to walking on eggs. You never know what shift in balance will break the delicacy of our day.

The previous two nights had been challenging for both Shane and his staff. My son had stomped his feet and screamed as he feverishly rocked in his recliner hard enough to put yet another hole in the wall behind him. With his hand, he had hit his face so hard and so frequently that it was still flushed in the morning hours. He had also been on the floor, banging his head against the hard surface. There are times when these events can last for hours. Or they may reoccur during a cycle over several days.

Prior to Shane's birth, I had a vision. How do you explain a vision? It's more than a dream, but it is a visual perception observed in a dream-like state of mind.

I was walking down steps, which lead from a large and magnificent church. The architecture of the structure was grand. I saw myself carrying a bundle wrapped in a baby blanket. I watched as I stopped at the base of the ascending stairs and lay the blanket away from the face of the bundled child. The face of a fawn was revealed. It had large, soulful eyes and tiny nubs which would grow into antlers, denoting it was male.

I knew my firstborn child would be a son. It would be many years before I could realize the depth and dimensions of the vision. My life was to change dramatically. My very foundations were to be shaken to the ground. My spirituality would be challenged.

David Shane Boldt was born on September 29, 1975, exactly on his due date. It was also my 29th birthday.

I had chosen the name Shane because of my childhood infatuation with the movie that featured Alan Ladd as the virtuous and handsome cowboy. The movie represented the simplistic and innocent times I had grown up in as a child. If my son would grow up to realize even half of the admirable traits portrayed by Alan Ladd's character, he would become a just and honorable adult.

My husband and I had originally planned on going out to dinner in celebration of my birthday, but the impending birth put a halt to our plans. I should have opted for dinner. Labor was intense. After repeated trips to the hospital, they finally admitted me. Three days later, the heartbeat monitor needle was repeatedly going off the end of the dial. My husband had originally planned to be present at the delivery, but they pushed him back into my room as they raced my gurney to the delivery room. I only recall attendants were pushing on my abdomen and hearing someone call out, 'forceps!'. I also heard someone say, "we almost lost him".

Shane spent the first hours of his life in the neonatal intensive care unit. When he was released from I.C., I held him for the first time. I was ecstatic. I told him we would have a wonderful life together. I recall telling him someday we would go fishing and learn the secrets nature had to tell. We would laugh together. I would teach him how to fly kites and ride a bicycle. I talked so much that my son must have surely thought he had chosen a babbling idiot for a mother.

Although he had poor sucking reflex and didn't eat well, he finally took enough nourishment to allow for release from hospital care. The attending physician told me perhaps Shane would be more comfortable in our home setting. He was sure that Shane would soon be a thriving infant. We were allowed to leave the hospital together. Several days later, my husband told me how he had read the 'registry' that was available to pacing fathers in the waiting area. The registry told of so many stillborns and difficult labors. We learned later that particular hospital had the highest infant mortality rate in the city.

The hospital did not release the birth records until several years later, when Shane was first entered into the world of special needs services. Because the records were necessary for a 'diagnosis' they were finally released, but not to me. However, they were shared by Shane's preschool. Finally I understood how very difficult his entrance into this world had been. Even with the traumatic birth, Shane was absolutely beautiful. He had fair, clear skin and intense brown eyes. There was an angelic quality to his looks, a brilliance and radiance.

Even as early as our arrival home I knew Shane was 'different'. The neighbor had a daughter 2 weeks older than my son. As most mothers, I compared her child's progress to that of my son. Shane slept for 10 or 20 minutes at a time, then would be awake for hours. He continued to have poor sucking reflex and ate very little. His pediatrician changed his formula to a soy based product, but the results were the same. Shane did not look at me, nor would he reach out for me. He had little to no interest in being held. Even as early as our first day at home, I knew something wasn't 'right'. There was an ever present, nagging feeling of foreboding.

From the instant you know your child is different, you will find yourself wearing a 'second skin'. It is akin to wearing a tight-fitting body suit, or sheath over your entire persona. This glove of concern will remain with you for the rest of your life, twenty-four hours a day.

Shane appeared alert and laughed, even at 6 weeks of age. A photographer who took one of our milestone photos together told me it was only coincidence that Shane 'posed' for the picture. He said no 6-week-old child could laugh and smile like he did. We ended up with some grand photos that show him 'posing', laughing.

It was at our 6-week infant check up a lady physician told me, "He's hydrocephalic. He won't live to be over a year old. You can get a second opinion if you like. See the receptionist.". With that she walked out of the room. As any confused and devastated mother would do, I made an appointment with a neurologist for that same afternoon. My husband met us there. We were assured that Shane was not hydrocephalic. The pediatric neurologist determined that Shane's head was well within the normal circumference range. However, he cautioned us there might be a need for him to monitor Shane in the months to come.

The early years were demanding and took their toll on the family. The older Shane became, the more evident it was that he was traveling on his own path, not the path taken by other children I observed. He crawled at an accelerated rate. When he took his first steps, he was running, not walking. He was hyperactive beyond any other children I had observed. He ate very little and was extremely 'picky' about what he would eat. By the age of 2 years, he could scale any piece of furniture, inclusive of the refrigerator.

He wasn't 'cuddly', but would often squirm and wriggle from my attempts to hold him. Clothing bothered him and he preferred to wear only diapers. Getting him dressed for any outings was a chore. He wasn't interested in the books I tried to read to him. However, when actually cornered, he could distinguish a circle from an octagon by pointing to the correct picture. I was comforted by the fact that he had an ability to discern small discrepancies. If he was that intelligent, then surely we could overcome any obstacles.

He thrashed about and turned over often. Sleep for Shane was elusive, save for the times he totally 'wore himself out'. He ignored my verbalizations to him and appeared not to hear anything I said. There were no coos or soothing 'baby' sounds. But he laughed a lot. There was no eye contact with me or anyone else. Yet, he appeared to be very alert and would smile for the camera when it was time to take milestone photographs.

As he grew, Shane appeared to enjoy riding in the car. If I was lucky, the movement of the car might lull him to sleep. When he was a little older than one year, I would point out (i.e.) cows. "What does the cow say?" We went through an array of animal identities and sounds, with no response. I wasn't to hear "Moo!" or any other response for many, many months. I also applied glitter around my eyes to encourage him to look AT me. That 'sort of' worked. He noticed the glitter with a confused look on his face, but at least I felt somewhat successful. It didn't matter that I had bent the rules a little in efforts to entice eye-to-eye contact.

He liked the rougher, tickling games, but was oblivious to my attempts to cuddle him. He would hold his arms outstretched and watch the movements of his fingers for long periods of time. He seemed to be pacing off the limits of his world and that world didn't seem to include me. He would stare at the walls, waving his arms as though he was attempting to distinguish his 'space' in the world.

Perhaps it was because he was so exceptionally handsome and 'normal' in his appearance. Perhaps it was because many young children do not talk until later years. The pediatricians we desperately sought answers from almost always told us they could not see that anything was wrong with our son. Other physicians told me I was just too anxious and worried. He was an only child and I was being too protective. If I did his talking for him, why would he have a reason to converse? In attempts to hear him speak, I would plead, coax and bribe him while he just laughed at me. I just wanted to hear him say

6

'Mommy'. I was not to hear that singular word for several more years.

He had no interests in the toys we would present. His only interests were in balls, leafing rapidly through picture books and running. He ran, bouncing off of walls whenever he could. He ran and screamed and laughed. If we attempted to generate an interest in 'quiet' activities such as coloring, the results were not positive. He didn't color 'pictures'. Instead, he used long, hard strokes of crayons with such intensity that they usually broke. If you said nothing and simply put the 'picture' on the refrigerator, it was O.K. If you praised him for the colors or what a fine job he'd done, he would rip the paper to shreds and laugh.

He had a distinct preference in food. We went through a period of several weeks when all he would ingest was the condiments stored in the refrigerator door. He lived on mustard, pickles, and jalapeno pepper juice. His pediatrician laughed at my concern and told me it was just a phase. I suppose it was because after four weeks he gradually integrated a few other selected foods into his diet. He did, however, remain very selective in his food preferences.

By the time he was 3 years of age, he could unlock any lock we placed on the doors. During the hours he was awake, he had to be watched constantly. My husband worked in construction and during the summer months the money was good. I was able to be a 'stay at home mom' for much of this time. During the winter months, I took a part-time job while he took care of Shane. I can look now upon those times and recognize the frustration my husband must have felt as a father. We couldn't 'get through' to Shane, who offered no affection, no warmth, in response to our attempts to work with him. My husband was distancing himself from any facsimile of family life, while I dove in deeper to be the 'good mother', the 'little

7

woman who stayed home and kept things together'. My son needed help and I had pledged myself to that cause. Looking back, I realize I had become an exceptionally driven and boring person.

My close friend Carolyn had been present at Shane's birth and was familiar with our situation. Being a teacher for many years, she had been exposed to special education students. She was concerned with Shane's progress, or lack of it. I can well remember the day she told me, "There is a condition called autism. But he won't be autistic. He just WON'T be!".

Autism was not as common then. As I was told, only 1 in 25,000 births was diagnosed as the child being autistic. We began our search for answers without knowing what questions to ask. I cannot remember how many 'second' and 'third' opinions we were to receive. No, he was alright. Well, he might have minor difficulties. There were no concrete answers. However, because he was lagging behind other children of his age on the developmental milestones, it was obvious there might be 'some' problems.

Shane was accepted into a program for children with an array of developmental disabilities. During our entry interview when a man came to lead Shane away from me, to undergo pre-entry tests. Upon test completion, he told me Shane had some skills upon command, but more interesting was that he reported Shane actually said, "I want mommy." I didn't believe him and wondered what sort of mind game he was playing. I didn't think it was possible because I had never heard Shane utter any words. Now, I do believe Shane spoke to him.

His teacher Beth was so enthusiastic and knowledgeable. She made his time at preschool 'fun'. Shane would occasionally take treats to school to share with his classmates. He seemed to enjoy passing out the potato chips, or whatever, to the others.

His teachers and aides felt that there was a problem, but with special education, most of his difficulties could be overcome. It was during an era the use of catch phrases like 'hyperactive', 'ADHD' and 'ADD' were common. I spoke with mothers who were dismayed because their child could not sit still, squirming constantly in their chairs. My son didn't sit at all for any length of time. More accurately, he would overturn the chairs as he raced past them. He was far beyond the 'squirm' stage.

Extended family members were concerned and adamant in voicing their beliefs that I should not have another child. What if a second birth would bring another challenging child into my life?

There was a second vision. *I saw myself walking, carrying a bundle wrapped in a baby blanket. When I stopped and turned the blanket to expose his face, there was a sleeping fawn, with the nub starts that would become antlers.* But I was not descending from the steps leading from a church in the vision. *The surrounding environment was that of a forest. In the background there were green trees and lush green grasses. I heard stream waters flowing. I saw myself smiling as I looked down at the young fawn I cradled in my arms. All was serene.* I knew I would have a second son. He would belong to this world.

Shane was 4 years of age when Miles was born. Again, labor was intensive. I lay there, thinking, "Here we go again!" and cursing loudly. Fortunately, the attending nurse was someone I knew. Her son had Downs Syndrome. He was in the same class at preschool with Shane. She pulled the doctor aside and explained the situation to him. He in turn spoke with my husband and me. Did we want delivery by Caesarian section? There was no doubt in our minds. Yes! It was later the physician told me I simply could not give birth by natural delivery.

As opposed to the angelic beauty of Shane, Miles came out looking like a red, wrinkled prune. But he ate well, slept well, cooed and was everything parents could want in a new bouncing bundle of joy! Within days, the prune vanished. We were proud parents of a beautiful male child bearing a delightful personality. Sans the prune façade, he was actually very cute.

For the most part, Shane ignored Miles. This wasn't unusual because he ignored his father and me as well. He simply did not appear to be interested in external stimuli or the environment around him. Even on Christmas morning we would urge him to unwrap his gifts. We would open his gifts for him, urging him to join in. We desperately tried every way we could possibly think of to get his attention. He was simply not interested.

After many physician appointments and a barrage of tests, Shane was diagnosed as having autism. The differences between his development and that of the 'regular' children were becoming very pronounced. It was an extremely painful time during which we longed for him to hit the milestones other children his age had already surpassed. Miles gave us coos and smiles in return for our cuddling, something we did not receive from Shane.

When Shane was five, we made the decision to move to Florida. The move was calculated to provide full-time employment for my husband. Also, we had heard good things about the programming for autism in that area. It was simply a case of the hoping the grass would be greener. We sold anything we had of value (antiques included!) and our family of four took our car, TomCat, a U-Haul truck packed with belongings, and our hopes southward.

Although my husband found employment, we discovered the programming for autism wasn't as advanced as we had hoped. Perhaps we were looking for miracles for all of us. Perhaps it just wasn't meant to be. Shane was enrolled in a preschool program for children 'at risk'. After only a few weeks, he was expelled. He was hitting the other children, for being uncontrollable, and for eating the recreation table. The staff said they just couldn't deal with him. The older he became, the more noticeable his 'being different' became. I clung to the fact that he was intelligent and very alert. Shane could name any picture in our collection of children's encyclopedias and picture books. This only occurred when he wanted to. Still, he offered no conversational speech.

My husband and I worked varying schedules, leaving little time for our ill-matched and strained marriage. During one last ditch attempt to spend some 'family' time together, we attempted a trip to Disneyland. Miles laughed and giggled at the sights and sounds. He was absolutely fascinated by the activities around him. The world was open to him. Shane scowled, screamed and kicked in his stroller. It was a devastating experience for him. It was as though we had sentenced him to a day touring Dante's Inferno.

Since his hearing appeared to be 'selective', we were referred for a hearing test. I still felt there had to be a very logical reason as to why he wasn't progressing with the normal stages of growing up. During the test, Shane sat alone in the testing booth. It was one of the few tests he has actually cooperated with. When the technician gave him instructions to pick up a pencil, a red block, a yellow block, paper, Shane would comply, choosing the proper object consistently. As the test came to the end, the technician turned off the equipment connecting the soundproof booth. The man and I were talking about Shane's perfect 'performance' in choosing the objects when we noticed Shane was still at task. When we would say, "he picked up the red block." he was continuing with the test, as per our 'unheard' conversation. The technician turned so Shane could not see him speak and continued instructions to him in low tones trailing to a loud whisper. And Shane continued to comply by selecting the proper items. He may have had difficulty hearing, but instead of having a deficiency, perhaps he was hearing too well.

If he could hear (i.e.) birds in the trees, cars on the street, our voices and a multitude of sounds simultaneously with the same intensity, how could he sort out the unnecessary sound stimuli? Was he hearing an accumulation of jumbled sounds?

His sense of smell also appeared to be affected. He would gravitate to odors which most of us found pungent and offensive with great interest and study. At other times, he appeared take note of smells which most of us could not detect. If he noted someone had washed their hair in a fragranced shampoo, he would follow them and, if they would allow, push his nose into their hair with smiles and satisfaction. This was particularly noticeable when an attractive young lady was the object of his inquisitiveness.

While in Florida, his pediatrician recommended he be placed on Mellaril. During the first weeks of this drug, I felt we had surely found a miracle 'cure'. Shane slowed down enough to pay attention a bit more often. He appeared to be somewhat calmer. The effect soon reached a plateau, but it was beneficial. It did not have effect on his mood swings, or in the sporadic aggression he displayed. In the years to come, we were to have new pediatricians who would be reluctant to change or discontinue this drug. Mellaril seemed to be actually effective for Shane. A decade later, we would be chastised because of our long-term use of this drug. The side effects from long-term use of any one medication can produce disastrous results. It was to be the first step in many years of trials and errors with medications.

It was also during our stay in Florida that Shane started showing outward aggression to me. I was driving while he sat in the front passenger seat. Suddenly he started hitting me for 'no apparent reason'. I pulled the car into the nearest parking lot. He stopped hitting and sat quietly. I heard him whisper an almost inaudible "Sorry.". It was at that point I began to encourage him to sit in the car's backseat, on the passenger side. Within the confines of the car the position allowed me to sit the furthest distance from him. I also purchased a 'special' seatbelt for him that he could not unfasten. It resembled a harness.

Relocation to Florida had been hard on the family. After a year and a half my husband and I agreed the marriage held no future for either of us. We parted amiably. He was to remain in Florida. He had a new network of friends, a steady job and I had our two sons and TomCat. I had no support system. I desperately needed the emotional support of my family and the security of familiarity.

Even now, I meet young mothers who ask if Shane's autism was the cause of my divorce. While I can say it wasn't the cause, it certainly didn't help. From the stories of young mothers, I hear the same theme of their devotion to the children and the strain it places on marriage. Do fathers have a more difficult time acknowledging their offspring are less than perfect? Does the maternal urge shift the mother's focus to turn all attention to the child in need? I don't have any answers. Eventually I was able to talk with my ex-husband. We agreed we had both married for the wrong reasons. We were good friends who had married and produced two offspring. Period. It had been a relationship built upon sand. We grew apart. Things happen. Today's divorce rate among parents of autistic children is, I am told, at 80%. But other people divorce, too. In today's chaotic world, it is difficult to maintain a marriage. Financial strains, work schedules, and personality differences are hard enough without additional strains. The needs of a disabled child definitely affect the entire family.

Recently, another mother and I were talking. We decided a number of fathers sought relationships away from the demanding household. Perhaps the burden of responsibility sets off the urge to be single again and recall their life, 'pre-child'. We laughed that so many a disillusioned husbands went into these relationships as a form of 'therapy'. Sometimes the therapy sessions can last all night, or days at a time, for their whereabouts are certainly unknown to their wives! Just to stereotype for a moment, mothers are usually the stable force within the family unit. We are probably Calvinistic in our attempts to create a stable household for our children. Yes, there are exceptions to this rule of thumb.

One of the most admirable men I have had the honor of knowing was a single gentleman raising his three children. The oldest was a severely autistic child who did not enter the group home system until after the age of 18. The last I knew, two of the children had grown to be responsible and respectful young adults. He remained devoted to them all.

I can only write my story from my view point because it is the only perspective I have. Also, there are so many more parents, mothers or fathers, who are raising their child as a single parent. That is indeed unfortunate. The person struggling with autism needs all of the heartfelt support they can get.

I returned to Indiana sans the U-haul, with only our smaller family of 3, TomCat, and all of the personal belongings our aged Volvo would carry. On the journey home, I ended up driving straight through the 1,100 mile trip. I attempted to stop at a motel about midway. I pulled the bed in front of the door so

Shane could not 'escape'. Miles slept well while Shane ran around the room giggling and throwing Gideon's Bible at the walls. There was no sleep for him or for me. As soon as Miles woke up, we resumed our trip 'home'. The weight of our belongings caused the Volvo's back bumper to scrape pavement over severe bumps in the road. Many hours later and thirty miles from home, the instrument gauges of our stressed vehicle were going absolutely crazy. The car would not go over 15 mph. As we finally pulled into my mother's back yard late one night, the car went belly up. Kaput. We were not to have a car for another two years.

We would live at my mother's house for the next few years. She worked, taking care of an elderly lady during the week. She was only home on weekends. Trips to the grocery meant waiting until Shane went to school. I would then place Miles in the traditional little red wagon and we would set off to the store. It was actually a lot of fun. During the winter months, we attempted to take a sled. Occasionally on the weekend, both boys enjoyed being pulled through the snow as we went to purchase a few items.

It was during our stay at mother's house that mild aggression from Shane began to increase. Miles was a playful and extremely imaginative child. He would pretend to be any one of an array of characters and Shane would be his comrade, or his adversary. He knew his brother was different, but we were living an isolated existence. Miles accepted Shane's rough play as being acceptable play.

My Aunt Mabel would take Miles to her home occasionally to play with the other children there. I am extremely grateful for this act of kindness and concern. One day this great lady and I were taking the boys for a ride in the countryside. On one particular road, someone had a sign in their front yard which stated, 'Doc's Place'. I was familiar with this area, but neither of my sons had been exposed to this area of the county. About a mile from this house, Shane clearly stated, "Doc's Place". It would have been impossible for him to see this farm because of the hills and wooded terrain of the area. Aunt Mabel and I just looked at each other. It was a glimpse into how he 'saw' the world. His perceptions were totally different than 'ours'.

Shane liked my aunt. Although he had brief exposure to her husband, he liked him as well. The first time he met Uncle Bob, he cradled my uncle's face gently in his hands and stared intently into his eyes for several minutes. It was as though he was reading his soul. When he removed his hands, Shane smiled at my uncle. He had accepted him wholly and completely. Bob took Shane for a ride on his garden tractor around the yard. Shane was enthralled. It is one of my favorite memories of that time period.

At about this age, we had to remove all mirrors and glass covering pictures from the house. Upon seeing his reflection, he would stare with an intense fixation, and then begin to beat his face and ears, screaming loudly. Whatever he 'saw' in the mirror or reflection was terrifying to him. Were there hallucinations? Or was it an extension of his 'reality'? I will never realize what he may have been seeing in his own reflection. Perhaps it was *something* other than his reflection.

By this point in his life, we had received evaluations from the best sources available. We stayed at Riley Children's Hospital for almost a week. The final report was an excellent psychological portrait of my son. There were no pat answers. We would have to wait until he was older to see just how severely he would be impacted by autism.

Shane went to his special education classes within the public school system. One day we were waiting for the school bus to pick him up. Talking to Shane was like trying to converse with a rock. To make sure he understood, I kept repeating his bus number (53) and giving him simple instructions. As the bus approached, I asked Shane if he could remember his bus number. He stated, "It's 53, Stupid!". I was ever so grateful for that complete sentence. Although he was by now expressing sporadic, simple one-word requests, it was the first complete thought he had spoken. I didn't even mind being called stupid.

Miles also had time away from Shane on the weekends when Grandma was home. She would walk downtown with Miles and stop for donuts and cocoa. He usually came home with a new toy or treats. There were children in the neighborhood who were Miles's age and their parents often invited him over to their house to play. Finally, there was some normalcy for Miles, at least in one small area of his life.

Miles slept well and kept a fairly 'traditional' schedule. Shane was victim to an erratic and light sleep pattern. I had to be awake to accommodate the sleep patterns of both boys. The only time I had away from Shane was during his hours at school. Respite programs, in those days, simply were not readily available. It wasn't a life. It was a marathon.

Of course I received all of the 'usual' advice from people who just wanted to advise. "All he needs is a good spanking.", "Bite him back and then he will stop!", "He's just spoiled rotten." were among the comments. Because he was such a handsome and 'normal' looking boy, people could not conceive there could be anything *really* wrong with or for him. They had no idea of the torment he experienced, nor how very hard we were trying to make things right for him.

Through a local agency, we discovered there might be limited respite care. The caseworker came to our home to interview, to evaluate us to determine if we would qualify for a few hours per month. As the caseworker and I sat at the kitchen table, I offered tea. The water was already boiling in a pan set on the stove. Suddenly Shane ran naked into the kitchen, bounded on top of the kitchen counter and urinated directly into the pan of boiling water. There had been no time to react or to stop him. She declined tea. I can look back on the incident and laugh. It was probably one of the most humorous and memorable moments of that time period. One has to develop somewhat of a black humor to cope with life sometimes. We were accepted as being a family in need of respite care (smile).

We interviewed a very nice lady for respite services. Yes, she had experience with behaviorally challenged children. One evening she took Shane out for ice cream while Miles stayed with a neighbor and her children. I actually had 2 hours away from both children. I went to the public library and walked around, not knowing what else to do with my time. The lady who had provided us with the respite care moved away the next week. I don't think we had anything to do with her leaving. There were no other workers qualified to provide time with Shane.

It was during this 2-year period that we tried our hardest to 'beat' autism. Previous allergy tests in Florida, and retesting when we returned to Indiana concluded Shane had shown allergic reaction in varying degrees to all foods except carrots and rice. Shane refused to have anything to do with either of these two foods. We started with the cave man diet, and then proceeded to a rotation diet. I feel we gave them all fair time in their trials. They were costly and used up any monies we had. I could not work because there was no adequate care for Shane. There was no child support for my sons forthcoming from their father. But we tried. The diets appeared to have no really noticeable effect on Shane. However, one day while on the rotation diet he had gotten into my purse and found chewing gum. He ate three sticks of the gum. Within the hour, he was wild, biting, screaming, thrashing. I could not get to the phone to call for help because of his relentless attacks on me. But it's just as well, for there really wasn't anyone to call. To this day, I do not allow chewing gum in his home.

We also noticed a slight escalation in aggression as a result of ingesting high caffeine beverages and chocolate. In the final analysis, it appears he is more allergic to environmental issues. He reacts to the world in general, and that is beyond our control.

I would like, even now, to know if allergy shots would benefit his condition. However, it is the allergist's policy to monitor patients for one hour after the shots, in case of adverse reaction. That is a reasonable safety precaution, but Shane does not tolerate the one-hour's wait. When forced to wait, for anything, he resorts to extreme forms of self-aggression and outward aggression. He has been known to attack anyone within range while biting and screaming. In some ways, he is his own worst enemy. As a final note on his allergies, mold is one of the worst offenders for him. Springtime, when the seeds and bulbs are bursting through the earth, is a remarkably difficult time.

Our hometown had no special education classes for autistic students. Shane was placed into a class for emotionally disturbed children. It was the best programming we could have had! The children were all verbal, but each with their own difficulties in life. They accepted Shane readily. They treated him as an equal, and he responded. His teacher was tolerant and patient. She was even good-natured when the other children urged Shane to stand up and say "bitch" when she walked into the room. While they would not dare to do such a thing, he was unaware such an act was not acceptable. He only realized the other children applauded his act of defiance. He had attained stature in the eyes of the other children. They accepted him and he beamed at their acceptance.

One afternoon after school, his teacher called me. She had noted that Shane had been naming the flashcards consistently wrong. She also realized that he was naming the flashcard behind the one being shown consistently. She mixed up the cards and again had the same results. He was naming the next card, not the one on top of the stack. In the days that followed, she repeated this activity. She also added another challenge, of putting cardboard over the text of a book he was not familiar with. He would read two to three words through the cardboard. She told me she was a good Christian woman and was only reporting what she had discovered, not that she believed it was possible.

We experimented with the books and flashcards at home. There were times when his accuracy at naming the unseen flashcard was 100%. At other times, he would ignore the cards completely. I don't know if Shane still has this ability. I don't challenge him. With the medications he has taken in his later years, I do not know if he has retained this ability. I do believe we all have abilities we are unable to tap into. I believe his brain was capable of rerouting some of the deficit areas to those areas yet to be explored.

I assume Shane learned some of his reading skills at school, but can't fathom exactly how that was accomplished. He certainly wasn't a model student (smile) and had absolutely no patience with the fine art of paying attention. I suspect he also self-taught himself some of his reading skills while rapidly leafing through the pages of his books and children's encyclopedias. Whether his ability is actually 'reading' or just word recognition, I do not know.

He was consistent in his ability to absorb everything going on around him without looking directly at the activity or the people involved.

That Christmas he actually unwrapped his gifts with some interest. He came to realize that the wrappings might conceal something he would like. I learned to only purchase items that he would be interested in. Clothing, balls, blocks, beef sticks and picture books still remain welcomed gifts.

While living in my hometown, I reconnected with an old high school friend. She accepted both of my sons with no reserve. They came to know her as their 'aunt'. One Christmas my friend 'aunt' Nancy had planned to have a Santa Claus come to her house to greet her nieces and nephews. She wanted Shane and Miles to be included in the festivities. I was a bit hesitant as I didn't know how Shane's hyperactivity and unpredictability would affect the other children. Finally, I decided we could stop in. Miles would be delighted and Shane should have an interest in the array of holiday edibles. We would only stay for a short time. The other children were in awe when Santa walked through the front door. Shane looked at him intently for a few minutes, then raced over to Santa and pulled his fake beard away from his face. He was overwrought with glee at having exposed the man's face from under the holiday facade.

Life at home was becoming increasingly difficult. When not at school, Shane would run around the house screaming and laughing. He preferred to wear little, if any, clothing and delighted in balancing and walking on the windowsill of the front living room's picture window, knowing it would upset me. His aggression to Miles, and to me, was increasing in intensity and in frequency. He would bite Miles on his arms. Their time together had to be closely monitored.

We learned of a school in southern Indiana that offered programming for children experiencing the same difficulties as Shane. I did not want him to move away from our family unit, but I knew we had to do something. He was accepted into their program. In an attempt to keep our family together, I made plans for Miles and me to relocate to the town where the school was located.

On the day Shane was admitted, Miles stayed with a neighbor while my cousin drove us to our destination. I cried throughout the entire 4-hour drive. I cannot remember even signing the paperwork to admit Shane. I do remember his new teacher, told us that he was 'so close' to coming out of autism. They would be able to do great things for him.

Back at home, Miles and I had our first taste of life without autism. We visited people, went for walks, shopped and actually came out of our isolation. I also made the necessary plans for us to relocate to the same town as Shane. If we lived closer to him, Shane would be home with us on weekends. He would remain at the school Monday through Friday. While the move took us away from my family support system, we made new friends soon after relocating. Miles went into a Headstart program, where he actually got to socialize on a daily basis with other children of his age group.

Because of repeated ear infections since infancy, a pediatrician recommended both Shane and Miles undergo surgery to have ear tubes installed.   It sounded like a promising idea, so I allowed for the surgeries to take place on the same day. Several weeks later, we learned both boys had perforated eardrums. The failure of Shane's surgery certainly may have been a result of his constantly beating and pounding on his ears. His right ear already had a cauliflowered appearance due to his self-injurious behaviors during his periods of ear infections and of being totally out of control. But Miles certainly did not hit his ears and the etiology of the perforation is still unknown. Miles had two subsequent surgeries to 'patch' the hole, but neither proved to be successful.

Shane's stay at the live-in school had been a positive experience for us, but it was only designed to be a short-term program. He had made friends with the teachers and the time during the week away from us was good for all of us. With regards to behaviors, he had not changed much. Shane was released and the three of us returned to live in a town closer to 'home'. We were back where we started.

Although the intense programming had offered structure and behavioral supports for Shane, he was still 'Shane'. He was getting older and the aggression escalated, both to Miles and to me. We had been through the parade of professional advice, medications, and behavioral specialists. Despite my adamant attempts to be consistent at home with the programs the school offered, he was becoming extremely violent and uncontrollable. He was brutal in his self-injurious behavior, occasionally 'ramming' his head into walls. He would beat his ears with his hands until they bled. I feared for his safety. I was also afraid for Miles.

After only five months of his being at home with us, I admitted him to a State hospital (institution) for children. Perhaps they could keep Shane from harming himself. I also needed to protect Miles, as well as myself. The first time I institutionalized Shane, I knew it would only be a short-term placement. He was on the waiting list for placement into a group home, a situation that I felt I could be comfortable with.

Prior to his admission to the hospital, we had yet another evaluation completed in Bloomington, Indiana. Indiana University's Resource Center for Autism is the finest informational center available. They left us with some excellent suggestions for working with Shane. I was able to pass on those suggestions to other programs he would be involved in. I would highly recommend the services this organization offers.

The programming at the institution offered support I could no longer give. There was socialization, structure, and around-the-clock care for Shane. He had the expertise of the intervention programming, physicians, aides, program coordinators and behavioral specialists. Shane continued to decline, behaviorally.

I tried to be as supportive as I could be. He now lived two and a half hours away from us. Every weekend we drove to visit with him. I sent notes with cartoons, treats, and occasionally spending money for the vending machines on site. I missed him terribly. There wasn't a night that I didn't fall asleep wondering how he was. Miles had given his favorite blue teddy bear to Shane for his stay there. It was soon 'missing' and I don't think Miles ever forgave the staff for the loss of his gift to Shane.

Shane attended public school away from the institution (hospital) during the day. The programming was excellent and Shane seemed to like school there. He wasn't attentive enough to work with some of the classroom projects with the other children. They created a special job he could perform independently. He would take mail and messages to the teachers in their classrooms. He took pride in his performance. It was creative and it worked for him. When the school added a new wing, he was chosen to be the ribbon cutter. I went to watch the ribbon cutting ceremony as he had been chosen to represent the school. He looked very proud as he posed with the school officials for the picture that would appear in the local newspaper.

Shane always excelled in activities that took him away from the group. Under aide supervision, he had a paper route in the afternoons. It was more of a local advertisement paper than a newspaper. It was his job to take the publication to the doorstep of each house on his route while his aide pulled a wagon filled with the paper. He did quite well on his route except when spotting a dog on his route. With that, he would scramble up the aide's body in attempts to get the most distance from the dog. It is good that he had the company of good-natured and patient aides.

I was ecstatic when the group home placement came through. He had been at the state hospital for a year. I believed the move to a group home would be permanent and would lead to his future placement as an adult. Of course when Shane moved, so did we. Miles and I had an apartment about thirty miles from him. Shane was there for a year, perhaps. I don't recall how long he had been there when they informed me they could no longer serve Shane. It didn't go well for him. I should have had the insight to take notice, for the proverbial handwriting had been on the wall.

It was not exclusively programmed for autism and most of the other children in the house were not autistic. I didn't care for some of the methods utilized. For example, while visiting one day, Shane was staring out the front window, tapping his hand against his leg. It was one of those involuntary actions a person will do when they are deep in thought. The manager came out of the kitchen, called for assistance and two adults immediately put Shane in a take down, restraint position while Shane screamed, bit and kicked. I protested, questioning why he would be restrained when he wasn't doing anything wrong. I was told that any form of body tapping or slapping commanded restraint. I didn't agree.

Again, he attended special education within the public school system. School was always challenging for Shane. There were times when simply transporting him to and from school was almost impossible. He had always seemed to like school buses. I will never know what he was trying to communicate by becoming aggressive to students. He was still considered to be non-verbal. Attempts to second guess the reasons as to why he was upset weren't often successful. The aggression during bus transportation occurred at various intervals during his years of going to public school. Perhaps it was because he simply did not want to be pushed into programming. Perhaps it was the noise level. He began to attack other students on the bus. There was a time when attacking children who could retaliate wasn't enough. He sought out the most vulnerable. He attacked children who were in wheelchairs. He also honed in on blind children. He calmed down somewhat when alternate forms of transportation were provided.

With Shane in full-time programming, I was able to accept full-time employment. Miles was in kindergarten and an excellent latchkey program for his time after school. Occasionally on the weekends, Shane would spend time with us.

He was becoming older and his aggressive streaks had become more intense. He could be laughing, playing with blocks one moment. The next moment, his pupils of his eyes would enlarge and become as black as coal. He would lunge at me in an aggressive flurry. Miles spent a lot of time in his room when Shane was with us. He knew when to run. Shane was losing ground and so were we.

Ultimately, he was expelled from the group home. They said he simply wasn't responding to their programming. They had tried for almost two years and weren't seeing progress. It is my personal opinion that Shane had not failed the programming, but that the programming failed Shane. After expulsion from the group home, we all returned to a town closer to home.

Life continued on its merry, bittersweet way. Shane was enrolled in a class for autistic children. Miles had started first grade. Somehow they managed to salvage a brother relationship. Among my prize possessions are pictures of Shane and Miles roller-skating down the hallway of our apartment. They would laugh and play, usually jumping on the beds and running through the hallway. Shane had a delightful sense of humor. He would tease Miles by putting jell-o into his brother's shoes and shaking it down into the toes. He would laugh when Miles put his shoes on only to discover Shane had gotten the upper hand…again. If I told the boys to clean up the back seat of the car, Shane would throw all of his papers and toys onto Miles' side of the car as if he were innocent of creating any mess. They were brothers and they were bonded.

One of my favorite memories is one night when the first snow of the season arrived. Miles was in the front yard playing with some neighbor children. Shane was staring out the window at the snowflakes coming down, illuminated by the streetlight. He had a wondrous smile on his face. He was absolutely enthralled by the sight and repeated "snow, snow". He wasn't watching the other children. He was simply delighted by the falling flakes. And I was delighted to actually hear him relate to the environment by speaking those few words.

One day Miles was watching cartoons. It was the show with the skunk who spoke with an exaggerated French accent. The skunk was saying "Oh ho ho". Shane happened to glance at the television. He repeated the phrase. I laughed as I asked Shane if he was Mommy's little Frenchman. That phrase would be repeated to me many times a day for the rest of his life. He says "Oh ho ho." and I repeat, "Oh ho ho. Mommy's little Frenchman.". Sometimes he will repeat the phrase with me. It is usually the first thing he says upon awakening if I am the person with him.

Another memory is quite tongue-in-cheek. Shane was still at the age when I could put him into the child seat of a shopping cart. One the few times we had attempted to shop sans the cart, he would run down the grocery aisles screaming "beer, wine!". I never could figure out where that came from. We were at the check out station and I was in the process of paying the cashier. Shane suddenly reached over and stripped my summer tube top down to my waist. He thought it was hilarious. I didn't. Somewhere along life's path with an autistic child, you simply shed the luxury of embarrassment.

Negative attention has always delighted him. It didn't matter how many compliments, candy treats, or positive reinforcement you offered. He just enjoyed the negative reaction as opposed to positive reaction. Try as you may to present a bland, no-reaction-whatsoever demeanor, he had an inner sense of just knowing you were upset. It was as though he could read your mind and your innermost thoughts.

Shane also delighted in smearing his feces, something he had done sporadically as a child. I tried to be consistent with each new endeavor to deter the behavior. We went through periods of time out. He had to sit still while I cleaned. Then I tried having him wash the walls while I supervised. The result was always the same. He laughed while I tried my hardest to present a blasé but firm front. He was always one step ahead of me. He was always one step ahead of the behavioral specialists. He was determined to address life as he chose and there wasn't a thing I could do about it.

But there were extremely dangerous times, also. The sporadic aggression had become harmful and intense. I was exhausted. There was little time for sleep and just monitoring Shane's extreme mood swings drained my energies. I felt it would only be a matter of time before one of us would be seriously injured during one of Shane's 'out of control' episodes. He was very capable of inflicting harm. Enough was enough.

In 1990, I faced the darkest times of my soul. I knew Shane would have to be institutionalized. The well of my inner strengths had been drained. I made arrangements for him to return to the State Developmental Center for children. After having tried so hard, for so long, I felt I had failed him. This placement would be permanent. There would be no reprieve for Shane. It was during those times I thought Miles would be better off living with his father and his new wife. Shane and I would be better off dead. I cannot describe the anguish of those days because there are no words which lend to the depth of my depression. From somewhere, strength came to go on. I had to accept Shane's anger with me. I am quite sure he was confused as to why he could not be with his family.

It was Miles who put the situation into an understandable perspective. He told me that if it was him, he would want to go somewhere away from the people he loved so he wouldn't hurt them.

Shane was readmitted to the state hospital. The days of moving from town to town to accommodate his programming and offer support to him were over. It was past time to put down roots, back to the hometown I had grown up in. Miles needed the stability of being able to grow up with some degree of normalcy. Financially, I needed to return to work on a full time basis.

Sundays were always open for my driving to the institution for visits. Holidays, also, were a day to spend with Shane. At Christmastime, Miles could awake early, open a few gifts, and then it was off to the institution, to spend the day with Shane. To this day, Miles does not appreciate the holiday season. It was a time not to be spent with ease and happy memories, but instead with the endless trips to the institution where Shane may or may not be happy to see us.

I did not allow Shane to visit home. The trip was over two hours long and it was no longer 'safe' to transport him any distance. I have been bit, hit, had my hair pulled out, and kicked in the head while transporting Shane. There were many, many times I was very afraid of my son's ability to hurt us during the times he was not in control of his actions.

At the hospital setting, Shane was now wearing a helmet full-time to protect his head when he would ram it into walls and furniture. He still bears scars. There are areas of his scalp that are barren of hair as a result of his self-abuse. He faired better than some who suffered from their own actions. The anguish suffered by so many people must be akin to the depths of some horrible, misunderstood hell. I have known people who have gone completely blind and, or deaf from self inflicted injuries.

His outward aggression was extreme. In those days before I had learned the fine art of 'duck and dodge', bruises and bites to me were prevalent. I've had my nose broken and experienced the unpleasantness of cracked ribs. It was usually the head-butting that inflicted the most damage.

The one time I had allowed Shane to visit over Easter weekend, he became very violent. For eighteen hours with no time for calming, he paced, screamed, and attacked me. At my orders, Miles had locked himself in his room and was not to come out unless I told him to. During this siege, Shane systematically broke everything in my bedroom. As soon as I could clean up broken glass from knick-knacks and pictures, he would break more. I called a friend who drove three hours to aid me in taking Shane back to the institution. I will never know the reason things went so badly that weekend. But I do know that at various time periods, he would say, "Move at home.". It wasn't until later I realized that meant something 'bad' was happening to or for him at the institution.

When Shane first left my care to go into programming, he would wear pajamas for bedtime, whether he slept that night or not. At some point during this time period, he started refusing to wear pajamas. He would become extremely agitated when asked to put on nightwear. I believe now that he was molested at some point and equates being molested with wearing pajamas. One thing I have learned in the past three decades is to understand things through his eyes. There is always a reason behind the aggressive outbreaks, and it is usually a logical reason. Sometimes the logical reason is medical in etiology. At other times, the logical reason is that *something or someone* is creating a situation he cannot handle. Finally the day came when he and I went through his belongings and threw out all of his pajamas.

Shane also lost the ability to 'share' with others. He did not interact with the other children. Many of his prized personal belongings came up 'missing' during his stay at the hospital. It appeared to be 'every child for himself' when it came to actually having anything they could call their own. Shane had learned to survive.

Although he lived at the hospital, he again attended public school off of the grounds. He had been fairly successful in the elementary school but programming had changed. In the name of progress, mainstreaming was introduced. Shane was to attend special education classes within a traditional school. The changeover seemed to be advantageous for some of the children. It was disastrous for Shane. He was also beginning the process of puberty.

His teacher told me during one particular lunch period, the basketball team had asked Shane to sit with them. They were not special education students. She said Shane sat at their table throughout lunch and beamed at his acceptance by the guys. But that was an isolated incident.

I visited the school unannounced as I could. It meant taking the day off of work and driving the five hour round trip to see him. His teacher had notified me that he was having difficulties and his aggression was becoming more pronounced at school. I went to his school. As I turned into his hallway, I saw him standing in the corridor. He was watching a young boy and girl walking by, holding hands. The show of any emotion is extremely rare for him. But tears were falling as he watched the young couple. He knew he didn't fit into the world around him. When your children hurt, you hurt. There was nothing I could do for him. There was no way to make it right for him. I waited a few minutes until approaching his classroom. He didn't need to know I had been there earlier.

It appears that intimate relationships are not a part of Shane's realm. He doesn't appear to make the connection of actually touching people in conjunction with a need for natural sexual gratification. If he were able to actually court a young lady and establish a consensual relationship, it would be nice and I would not be opposed to him establishing that bond. However, that will never be a part of his life. It is my understanding most persons with autism do not experience a need for physical relationships. But with that said, he has always had an eye for and a weakness for 'pretty ladies'.

During swim class, he was known to occasionally make an inappropriate grasp at one of the young female instructors. The girls were pretty good-natured by his gestures. He would burst into laughter. We weren't sure if his acts were due to his negative attention seeking behaviors or if it was simply the dragon of puberty rearing its head.

Ultimately, he was expelled from special education for his severe aggressive outbursts. I think that was when he was a high school junior. I could have fought for an S-5 for him to attend 'an appropriate' school out of state. I chose not to pursue the matter. For all I knew, I could have been putting him into a worse situation and I would not have been there to monitor. He was not the only student to be expelled. Mainstreaming had not worked for several other residents of the institution.

The state hospital chose to school Shane and a few other students within their building. It didn't appear to be very organized, or very educational. I think they watched a lot of movies and colored a lot of pictures. One day I made one of my surprise visits to see him. As I walked past a classroom, I saw a young man standing with his face against the blackboard. A tall male aide was punching him in the lower back as the boy screamed. It was my son. I reported the incident and demanded an investigation. I don't know how their investigation turned out. The only witnesses had been several non-verbal children and me. I was told it was not the center's policy to share investigation reports with the parents.

I will never know what he did endure during his time away from me as a child. I do not need to know details. Life is hard enough as it is.

I would note that by this stage of his life, he had an earned reputation of being 'non-compliant' and unruly. While I do not attempt to know how Shane perceives the world, I do attempt to give him the benefit of doubt. Playing devil's advocate has always been one of my favorite games. Suppose he was trying to say, "I don't want to be there because something (or someone) frightens me.". And suppose he were *thinking* those words, but *all that we could audibly distinguish* was "dwagommme". Suppose he had a migraine and wanted to tell someone, but all that came out of his mouth was, "aaaahdur". He truly thought he was telling them correctly, but that they were ignoring him.

If I were him (or if I were just me), I might, as a last ditch attempt, desperately call attention to my needs by finally taking drastic measures to gain recognition. But it wouldn't matter, because no one had an idea of what I was trying to communicate. In Shane's eyes, we would be 'non-compliant' and disrespectful of what he needed. So, have we taught non-compliance and disrespect by role modeling? Why would we not expect the same from him?

Even before Shane's 18th birthday, we had started the paperwork trail to have him transferred closer to home. The Developmental Center for adults was thirty minutes from our home. The previous drive was two and a half hours, one-way. We could visit more often and offer family support more frequently. It wasn't until later that I was informed he could have been transferred prior to the age of 18.

On the day his previous facility transported him to his new home, we were there to great him, support him, and of course, sign the paperwork. He arrived in a white van with several staff. He looked so gaunt, so frail, and vulnerable. He arrived with the imprint/mark of a man's shoe on his chest, right in the middle of his white t-shirt. Someone on the van had kicked him en route.

While the new staff gave him a wheelchair ride around the grounds, a lady approached me. She said she understood how I felt and knew what I was experiencing. I learned later that she truly did understand. Her severely autistic son was just a few years older than Shane. Her kindness and sincerity was appreciated more than she could ever realize. We had no way of knowing at the time that she would prove to be Shane's guardian angel. I didn't know at the time, but I would come to owe her more than I could ever repay.

The following years remain somewhat of a murky, busy blur for me. Again, the institution offered structure, socialization, and constant programming. Professional staff was available, inclusive of doctors, nurses, behavioral specialists, and programming specialists. Again, there was no improvement in his behaviors or frequency of his mood swings and cycles.

Every so often there would be an investigation when I complained of noting marks on Shane that he could not have imposed on himself. Of course no one was ever found to be 'guilty' of the marks. There was numerous extremely excellent direct care staff. The performance of only a handful of staff was questionable. Shane has an innate ability to judge people. He would rely on the biggest, most compassionate staff he could find and cozy up to him. He would also bond with the gentle, yet firm personnel. He had learned the survival skills. His sleep habits didn't fit into the program and he would often be up at night, eating popcorn with staff and watching television while the other clients slept. He slept a lot during the day programming. It appeared he genuinely liked many of the people who worked with him. He did not bond with the other people living there.

While at the Center he became fast friends with one of the staff, a man close in age to Shane. They did 'guy' things together and Shane reveled in 'being accepted' by this energetic young man. They shared common interest in cars, music, and young ladies. The man gave Shane a poster of a lady posing in a bathing suit and posted it in his room. Shane thought it was great. It wasn't long before an 'unknown' female staff removed and destroyed it because she thought it was demeaning to women. He was allowed to have possessions, as long as they were 'acceptable' to his caregivers. People were always imposing their own beliefs on Shane. It must have added even more confusion to his life. When he made attempts to express his own interests and thoughts, his efforts were thwarted by the conflict of others' interests. In an act of self-righteousness, the female staff had violated his Rights.

Shane preferred to wear his hair long. It wasn't exactly an 'in' style at the time. The long hair of the 1960s was long past and it wasn't a time for 'mullets' either. It was, however, his choice and I supported him wholeheartedly. When and if he wanted his hair cut, he would somehow let us know. One day I walked into his room. He was sleeping and his long hair, still bound by a rubber band, was lying in the wastebasket. Someone had cut his hair. I came unglued. What was it about Human Rights they didn't understand? There was an investigation, but no one stepped forward to admit the act. If they had, I certainly was not to be informed. Later, one of the female staff told me that it looked better anyway and that she certainly liked his hair short. Human Rights may look good on paper, but unless the direct care truly understand and respect them, they are worthless.

For a while, Shane had a communication board. It was a marvelous model and he was able to utilize it. He would occasionally type words independently, without being touched in any manner. It was only when he chose to 'perform' and he would not usually type if asked. The machine printed out in a ticker-tape type of paper. His instructor showed me five words he had selected one day. I can only recall three of the five words. They were 'Chrysler, Mommy, and Cheezburger'. Somewhere along the line, that machine 'came up missing'. While being in the care of others, many of his belongings grew legs and walked off into oblivion.

Occasionally we attempted home visits. One such Sunday I picked him up. Before driving home, we stopped at his favorite fast food restaurant to get the sandwich he had requested. We had placed our order and I pulled the car forward in line to wait for our food. Suddenly Shane slammed his head through the car window closest to his seat. Being a quiet Sunday morning, there were few cars on the streets. That was good because I couldn't have driven him back to the institution any faster than I did. The nurses checked him thoroughly for injury to his face and ear. While there were a few fragments of glass on his face, he had escaped serious injury. Staff at the Center advised me not to take him home because they feared he might have another 'episode'. But Shane was sheepish and sat there quietly. I could see the incident was over. We drove the thirty miles home with the wind whipping through the space where our car window had been. We had a very nice afternoon.

Shane also benefited from positive experiences while at the Center. When 'all systems were go', he actually enjoyed going for van rides with other patients and an occasional community outing. Going to the movie theater didn't hold his interest and he usually left before the end of the show. However, he did wholeheartedly enjoy concerts and 'live' performances. On one occasion, a famous singer impersonator came to the Center to give a rock performance. Shane stood directly in front of the stage in awe and was perfectly still for the entire show, except for applauding at the end of each song.

Shane's 'group' and staff also went to the large coliseum in his town to watch a live performance. Staff in attendance said he seemed to enjoy the show. However, when the show was over and the house lights came on, he was absent. He had slipped away undetected. I'm glad I wasn't in attendance; I would have been frantic. The staff felt it was best if they took the rest of the group back to the Center before they continued their search for Shane. When they got to the bus that had transported them to the event, he was waiting for them. There had been hundreds of cars in the parking lot. He had navigated through the night, the traffic, and the sea of vehicles to safely find his ride to the Center.

There were to be two more occurrences of his going off on his own. Both times he was found walking and looking at houses in neighborhoods several blocks away from the Center.

I was employed with a provider agency that served developmentally and mentally challenged persons. I can look back and honestly state it was probably one of the most sincere agencies I have viewed, or worked with. I have noted agencies in smaller towns appear to have better knowledge of what exactly is going on in the consumer's home and with their activities. Although community resources are limited in smaller areas, there appears to be a 'family' atmosphere among the administration and direct care staff. It appeared they worked with the consumers, as opposed to 'at' them.

My job role with the agency was as a job coach. Later I assumed the role of a community integration specialist. Both positions were geared to aid developmentally developed and mentally challenged persons assimilate into the community. I liked the people and positions there. But it was a constant reminder as to how much more severe Shane's behaviors were as opposed to the other people I served.

I learned of an innovative new technique to aid individuals with autism - Auditory Integration Therapy, or AIT. The purpose of the therapy was to desensitize the ears and stimulate the cilia within the ear canal. The listener wears earphones, hearing a wide range of sound as he listens to various musical selections.

One of the administrative staff where I was employed learned of my desire to have Shane experience AIT. She presented the request to her sorority, who ultimately funded the venture. We were to be in Ohio for one week while Shane received AIT on a daily basis. Another employee of the company received permission to accompany. He would be paid for his time. The man was an assistant youth pastor, was active in his church, and appeared to be dedicated to the population he served.

Auditory Integration Therapy went well. Shane wore his earphones and listened to the music/tones when directed to do so. He was surprisingly cooperative. During one session, he was eating a small bag of corn chips and said quite loudly, "I don't even like these!". On the last day there, he head butted a large hole in the drywall. Our therapist was extremely patient and understanding. When a colleague asked her 'why' she would attempt to administer therapy to people who were so severe, she had replied that these were the very people who needed it the most.

For the week we stayed at the hotel, the man who went with us watched Shane while I slept, and vice versa. One evening he stated he had to make a personal trip home. He was to return the next day. After he left, Shane's 'behaviors' started to escalate. Two hours later he was in the middle of a horrible 'full-blown' episode. The hotel management received numerous calls from other guests reporting someone was 'beating a child' in our room. His running, screaming, and throwing himself against the walls had awakened two floors of hotel guests. He showed no signs of slowing down and I called EMS to transport us to a psychiatric unit. As soon as we entered the back of the ambulance, Shane hung his head and began to cry. He became very quiet. Upon arrival at the unit, he fell asleep while holding my hand. The attending physician was very nice, but he couldn't understand why I was still trying to help Shane. He told me I should return Shane to the institution and walk away.

AIT didn't appear to 'do wonders' for Shane during the sessions, but a surprising event happened when we returned to the institution grounds. While walking from the car to his dorm, one of the patients bumped into him. Shane responded by speaking a full sentence; it was witnessed by those of us closest to him. I will never forget what he said. It is one of only ten or twelve complete, complex sentences I have heard him speak. He said, "Excuse me. You grazed my arm.".

Only a few months later at work, I was called into the personnel director's office. She is one of my favorite people. She's a neat professional lady who faces life with honesty and humor. As gently as possible, she told me the man who had accompanied us to Ohio had been arrested. One male member of his church youth group had named him as being a child molester. Other boys came forward, also. The man was evidently putting sleeping pills into the boys' beverages while they spent time with him. While under interrogation, he had also admitted to 'fondling' Shane. It was one of those moments the floor goes out from you and you feel suspended in confusion. I asked her how this could happen. I had been in the same room with Shane when he was there. She was very kind and gentle. She said, "But you slept.". Hence, the reason for the trip to the psychiatric ward was revealed. Shane was trying to tell me. I could not decipher his cries.

Had it not been for the actions of this 'man', Shane probably would not have head butted into the drywall on our last day at AIT. Had the whole of the experience not been so traumatic for him, I would have tried to attend more sessions. I find AIT beneficial and believe the recipients do receive positive results.

Because he was a resident of the soon-to-close State Developmental Center, he received some priority on the waiver program waiting list. He would go under the care of an agency, in a real house, with real choices. At least that is how I perceived it at the time.

With weeks to go until his release from the Center, he suffered appendicitis. It was later learned his appendix had been burst for about two days before he was taken to the emergency room. How could someone be so visually ill without any staff taking notice? One of the nurses at the Center was the very person who had welcomed us on our first day there. This grand and kind lady had just walked into his 'dorm' one night. She took one look at Shane and immediately called an ambulance to transport him to the hospital. Then she called me. I met them at the emergency room. It was determined he would undergo immediate surgery. He was gravely ill. After surgery, he was admitted to intensive care and then to a room. No one was sure if he received medical aid in time.

As I stayed in the hospital with him, I was very aware he may cross over. I watched over him, realizing just how short life can be for some people. I also realized how very long life can be for others. I gave him my permission to cross over if that was what was intended. I watched him sleep, wondering if our time together was at an end. He had suffered within his prison for his entire life. He had spent his life attempting to fit into a scheme he didn't understand. I was willing to let go.

In the following days, he began to show improvement. He liked getting shots because it meant the pain would subside. He was actually cooperative, to a point. It took a great many helium filled balloons to amuse him. It was harder for him to 'pop' them and it did occupy some of his time. Even now he actually likes shots and blood draws.

During our stay at the hospital, an investigator from Indiana Protection and Advocacy Services interviewed us as a part of their investigation into why Shane had not been admitted to the hospital sooner. The lady who came was a seasoned mother herself. Her son had Aspergers Syndrome, a high form of autism. Her honest candor and vast knowledge of autism was a great relief. We became good friends. Although she now lives in another state, we can occasionally communicate via e-mail and phone.

One of the greatest difficulties children with disabilities brings to our lives as mothers is that dealing every day with the child's needs AND dealing with the government and agency systems that we ARE reliant on for survival leaves us exhausted and vulnerable. This 'vulnerability also leaves us open to instinctually bond with another 'warrior' walking a similar path. This creates a much deeper relationship that can span years and space.

Because our childrens' lives differ so much from typically developing children, we are often left out of school and after school activities, traditional Parent/Teacher gatherings and god knows we have no time for bake sales. Yet mothers of children with disabilities DO find each other and assist each other by shoring each other up and sharing information. Instead of meeting in car pools or in the bleachers for a child's sporting event, we meet each other at the hospital, the agencies, and the public hearings. We instantly recognize each other. Instead of discussing grades, the accomplishments of our young men, every day gossip, and trading recipes for crock-pot dinners, we share recipes for survival.

Now both of our sons are older. During my friend's occasional visits home, I try to meet with her for laughter and a glass of wine. We always address the plights of our sons. Then we can move on to giggle about world events, politics, love, life, and which way the wind might be inclined to blow.

It was also during our post-appendectomy in the hospital when I received an 'anonymous' phone call from a lady. She said she worked at the Center and, if I valued my son, I would not allow him to return there. She cited horror stories of his being forced to eat his own feces, being sexually, verbally and physically abused. Shane had been gravely ill and now this! I was extremely grateful Adult Protective Services was already represented. Now they were at ground level for yet another investigation into the allegations.

I called the Superintendent of the developmental center, a man I held in high regard. He was a man in an administrative position, but he had taken time to know each resident's name. He greeted every person personally when making routine inspections of the dorms. He knew the habits of each person and what could be expected in their realm of behaviors. He stated he would initiate an internal investigation. Subsequently, several persons were suspended while allegations of any abuse were to be proved, or disproved. Ultimately all persons were brought back into service, with back pay. I will never know if the allegations were true or false. I do not need to know. Shane had only a few weeks to live at the institution before he would enter a service provider (agency) home.

Shane did return to the Center after his release of the hospital, but was taken to a different building, with different direct care aides. One of our close friends, Miles, and I returned to Shane's original dorm to gather the last of his possessions. When we carried his belongings to our car, several staff who had worked with Shane were present. They blocked the exit with their bodies, refusing to move. No words were spoken as we pushed past them. The investigation had brought some of their own under scrutiny. We were not welcome there. Those particular people were extremely hateful to us. That was our exit from the Center.

Several weeks later, Shane moved into a house rented by the agency we had chosen to oversee his care. He would soon be joined by a roommate before a third gentleman would join them. He didn't know the staff and he certainly did not know what to expect from the move. I was adamant about being at the house during his first night there. I would stay in the garage, but would be available in case staff couldn't understand his requests or had any questions about his care. The staff who came didn't know Shane and she wasn't interested in knowing him. She knew I was present, but did not know I could actually observe the scenario from the garage. She talked on her cell phone, watched television, and played video games while Shane ran throughout the house. He ran rampant, screaming and laughing hysterically. The ordeal went on for hours, but she didn't budge from her seat on the sofa. The next day I was adamant that particular lady was not to be scheduled to work with him again.

Within days, more experienced (or more professional) staff were introduced. It was a confusing time for Shane. He had not lived in a house since he was a child. His roommate moved in several weeks later. He was a young man who had also lived with Shane at the Center. They were poorly suited to live together. The young man chosen to live with him was deathly terrified of animals, even pictures of them. Shane loved stuffed animals. He would run into the living room holding his stuffed owl and stop directly in front of his roommate. He would push the owl into the young man's face and say "Owl! Owl! while laughing. That would set the young man into a rage of screaming and throwing himself into walls. Shane was not especially kind when letting his dislike for roommates be known.

He had learned to survive at the Center by interacting with staff and ignoring the other residents. It appeared he had not even particularly liked most of the other people living at the Center. In this setting, he was forced to actually interact with the young man in close quarters. It was a disaster. Shane was head butting into the wall on a daily basis. I think the record number of holes in the drywall was six in one day. It soon became apparent he needed to live solo. It was also apparent he required double staffing for twenty-four hours a day, seven days a week, to prevent him from seriously injuring himself.

Prior to the agency finding a new home for Shane, there were many more incidents. There would also be many more trials with finding good matches between him and his direct care people. I am very pleased he has the gift of assessing people.

One male staff came to us, delighted he would have the opportunity to work with an autistic person. He expounded his virtues. I liked him. He preferred the gentle approach. He could play his Indian flute for Shane, as well as entertain him with his guitar. I clearly recall him stating that he didn't believe in anger and that his Buddhist training made him an excellent candidate to work with Shane. But Shane kept his distance, eyeing him suspiciously and 'sizing him up'. During an outing several weeks after his introduction to this gentle man, Shane evidently decided to dig to the core of this man. In an aggressive flurry, he began attacking the man. Shane also started ripping off his own clothes while screaming loudly. Understandably, the staff pulled the car over and got out. But he had left the car in neutral. The car rolled across two lanes of traffic before settling in a shallow ditch. No one was hurt, but I have to smile at a visualization of the scene. There had been a naked man climbing and screaming in the ditched car while another man paced outside.

Two days later, we had a meeting at the house to discuss new strategies. This kind and gentle staff sat across the table and hatefully glared at Shane during the entire meeting. If looks of hatred could kill, we would all have died that day. Several days later, Shane hit the man. The staff left the house in a huff, tearing the garage door opener and house numbers off of the house in his haste.

Additional staff were introduced to the house. One male direct care instantly became the target of Shane's moods and behaviors. I couldn't understand why Shane was testing him so adamantly. I didn't think the male staff would last two weeks. His name was L.G.; he is still with us, six years later. We've since laughed about my thoughts that his longevity wasn't worth two cents.

Somewhere in this time period, I had acquired a job with the State at the Bureau of Developmentally Disabled (BDDS). The office is the 'gateway' to the placement of people into provider service situations. It was a pleasure to work with the staff there. They were professional and friendly. They were also fun to work with. I still attempt to stay in touch with several of the people there; they bring a sincere smile to my day. My position was as a quality monitor, with the primary duty being the performance of surveys. My counterpart and I visited provider service homes to check for State compliance. We also completed surveys to determine if the consumers and families were satisfied with the placement. I would remain with State for almost five years.

I also returned to school. I started classes at a State college to become an LPN, but soon switched the curriculum to massage therapy. In two years, I had a technical degree in medical assistance. Later, I began classes at another college with the high hopes of eventually attaining a degree in Anthropology. Other than that, the years were relatively uneventful. Both of my sons were growing up. Miles was making his way through high school.

Miles and I took the opportunity to experience two vacations during those years. We spent time at Florida's Disneyland campground, enjoying everything we could cram into the week. Several years later, we took a train trip across country to Arizona. I had been to the southwestern states several times (pre-marriage) and wanted to share the love I have for that area with Miles.

I was in my mid-twenties when I first drove through the area surrounding Flagstaff. For reason unknown, I had to pull the car over, being totally overwrought with emotion. I felt as though I had 'returned home', although I had not traveled in that particular area before.

Miles and I spent the week exploring mesas, canyons, ancient ruins, and anything else we could do for our short period of time there. Miles was getting older and was maturing handsomely. I felt it would be our last vacation together before he reached adulthood and ventured off to explore his own path in life.

By 2003, it was apparent Shane was losing ground, neurologically. He walked slower and his gross motor skills appeared to be declining. It was also evident that he had not, and probably would not, conform to the programming he had been exposed to for so many years. Shane remained steadfast in his determination to do things 'his way'. I may never know if it is totally due to autism, or if there may be just a touch of 'bullheadedness" present.

Service provider (agency) homes usually had two to four people living in each house. During my years with State, I monitored the available paperwork and services that were presented to the homes. Now I wanted to know exactly how they operated, internally. I was hired as a supervisor to be in charge of several houses.

Within weeks, I regretted taking the position. With my own son in the system, I looked at the clients through the eyes of a parent. I wanted the clients to be heard, their needs to be met. I learned appearances can be very deceiving. I also learned that even as supervisor, you really have no control over what happens when you are not physically present. In addition, many of the institutional settings have closed, or are closing. The population flooding into group/waiver homes is overwhelming.

Other than a few 'minor' incidents, life went on rather uneventfully for Shane. He was now living in a nice home and had assigned double staff on a full-time basis.

We were in his allergist's office when the nurse happened to notice Shane's profile. With the light coming through the window, she noted it simply didn't appear to be 'right' and advised us to have his eyes checked. I was sure nothing was wrong because he had a complete physical complete with dental and vision prior to his release from the Center. His eyes 'track' and follow move together perfectly. I had no idea there was a problem.

We contacted the specialist who told us Shane had a cataract and was totally blind in his right eye. He could undergo surgery, but there was a chance he may self abuse, causing permanent blindness. There could be no post surgery trauma. Since he could not see from the eye anyway, I decided we would risk the surgical procedure. We would add Valium to his already heavy medication regime during the weeks of recovery to avert self-abuse.

I was so sure he would regain his sight. I was genuinely convinced nothing could ever harm my son again. It wasn't meant to be. Shane's retina had been detached from his years of self abuse. Even without the cataract, he would be permanently blind in his right eye. I can only surmise he beat his hand against his eye in attempts to communicate the loss of sight as the cataract developed. It had been chalked up as a 'behavior'. Because he could not communicate his fears, he had been physically and medically restrained instead of receiving crucial medical assistance.

How many times did Shane have to be mentally and emotionally cut off at the knees before he could no longer stand? His ability to adapt and survive is more than admirable.

In regards to autism, I believe the word 'behavior' should forever be changed to 'communication difficulty'. Perhaps then people would begin to offer valid help to our autistic population. EVERY 'behavior' Shane has is due to his inability to communicate a medical or environmental event.

I had learned about a home program with a service provider company that allows for unique services. The program, I was told, allowed the parent to be in control of direct care personnel. It was my understanding we could be truly creative with Shane's programming. I could create an environment of optimum safety and health. I would be in a position to monitor his everyday activities. We interviewed with the company to determine if we were to be a good match for them and ultimately were placed on their waiting list. It would only be a matter of time before we could offer truly beneficial programming to Shane.

While we were anxiously waiting to begin our new lives, he remained under agency care. Several noteworthy incidents occurred during that time. A supervisor had called me to come to Shane's home one day. While Shane was supposed to be receiving double staffing, there had been a troublesome development. One of the staff worked another full time job and slept while he was supposed to be working with Shane. The other staff had been attending college classes during working hours (and being paid). They were simply covering for each other while Shane was, for the most part, ignored. In addition, three days of medications errors were detected. Shane had not received vital medications for three days. Although the medication documentation sheets had been initialed, his medications were still in their bubble pack containers. There had been major negligence in his care.

On another occasion, I had received a phone call from the supervisor of his house. Upon turning onto his street I could see several police cars in his driveway. Inside, two detectives and five policemen were attempting to hold Shane positioned so that they could take photographs of injuries on his body. He was fighting and screaming. I believe he thought they were going to restrain him. Even with his history of self-abuse it was obvious the injuries were inflicted from an external source. His back was scraped and the skin was raw. It appeared as though someone had dragged him across the carpet by his feet. There were bruises on various parts of his anatomy. There were marks that looked suspiciously like they could have been inflicted with a belt.

Shane has never had a good command of pronouns. When the detectives would ask him "Who did this?", Shane would respond by saying, "You did it.". Since the men had never met Shane until the day the supervisor summoned them, they had a pretty good idea he would be of no help with the investigation.

Everyone who had worked during the week was investigated and questioned. I believe the detective involved questioned two of the men on more than one occasion in attempts to identify who had actually perpetrated the abuse inflicted on Shane. The only staff determined to be innocent were the men who had not worked that week. The agency's staffing schedule mandated two staff were to be with Shane one week, and then they would rotate with another team of two persons who would work the next seven days.

The detective leading the team could not have been nicer or more professional. He kept me informed. The men continued with their pleas of innocence and it was impossible to determine who had been the perpetrator. I believe one man was eventually fired for other allegations. Another staff that had been

50

investigated quit. My gut instinct told me the man who quit was probably innocent. But he had 'gone down' with the rest of them. I insisted none of the possible suspects were to work with or even be around Shane again. One man was transferred to another home. He was the staff who had taped his own television show preferences - over Shane's very personal and prized VHS tapings of his favorite show. We were, and are, unable to replace those tapes for Shane. I was happy to be rid of that staff, regardless of his possible innocence or guilt in the abuse case.

When a staff frightened or intimidated him, Shane would often be very quiet and attempt to maintain a healthy distance to that person. But he would inevitably take out his feelings on people he could 'trust'. Several of us bore the blunt of his physical outbursts if he could not, or *would* not, act out on the person he didn't like. I suppose it was a take on the old song, 'You Always Hurt The One You Love'. However, that brought little comfort to those of us who were targeted.

The decline of Shane's neurological functions continued, although not at a steady rate. It was at the spiral and plateau stage. Subtle changes in his gait and balance were noticed. Since there had been a long period of negligence, it was impossible to determine if any health issues had been contributing factors in his loss. It would be at a future time that I would suspect Shane may have had at least one grand mal seizure during the time he was being ignored.

During one routine visit to one of his respected physicians, Miles and Shane left a few minutes early to go to the car. This physician is one of the wisest and most compassionate persons I have ever had the pleasure of meeting. I needed to ask questions that could not be asked in Shane's presence. I asked if he felt there was a particular etiology to the obvious decline. Instead of answering directly, he asked me what I thought it was.

I told him I felt Shane was losing ground and there wasn't a damned thing we could do about it. He looked at me silently for a few moments and then said, "Yes, I believe you are right."

It was a team decision to have Shane's medication regime re-evaluated. He had been on Valium since his eye surgery and we were beginning to notice adverse side effects. We would have to decrease the dosage a little at a time until he could adjust. It did not go well. He stalked the house in a zombie-like trance saying "take pill…take pill". He broke down the door to the room where the medications were locked. He threw his head into the walls. The psychiatrist we had urged us to put Shane into an inpatient program fifty miles away. It was quite an entourage. Shane's case manager, behavioral specialist, two staff, Miles, I and Shane drove to the clinic where he was to stay throughout the withdrawal process. Miles and staff stayed with Shane while I gave the intake coordinator pertinent health/history information. Almost an hour into the interview, I began to have serious concerns about their programming. I could observe and hear the other patients. They were all verbal and appeared to be functioning without the burden of autism or mental diagnoses which plagued Shane. They were in patients only to facilitate withdrawal from street drug usage.

IF Shane was cooperative, he could make a phone call home at the end of the week. IF he was cooperative and adjusted to the program without incident he could have monies to buy a snack. What part of severe autism did these people NOT understand? I was cringing and having third thoughts about the appropriateness of the setting when Miles approached me. If I didn't take Shane home right now, he would. Shane had been running around his 'room' crying "go home now" repeatedly. Our entourage went home, with Shane. Yes, he would go through withdrawal. But it would be in his home, with the support of his people. Ultimately, we (all) survived throughout the duration of his withdrawal period.

The months of waiting to become providers under the home service providers ended. We would soon to have a 'family' program. Shane had been in programming since the age of four. He had been in day programming, semi-permanent programming, the institution, and under the umbrella of agencies. The new programming would be something he had not experienced before.

While Shane had been on his own path, Miles and I had enjoyed the opportunity to have somewhat of a 'normal', single parent life-style. Miles was now in college. I had returned to college. With the decision to serve Shane in a home setting, I made the conscious choice to bring an abrupt halt to my studies. I chose to spend the next years taking care of Shane on a daily basis. It was simply a matter of priorities. Shane needed me more than I needed a degree. We had waited too many years for the opportunity to do it 'our way'. I had spent too many years wondering how he 'could be' if offered an alternative situation. Now I would have the opportunity to know.

In retrospect, I am comfortable with the opportunities the past years of programming had afforded. Had we not made those choices, he would not have had the opportunity to experience socialization, structure, and constant programming. It just didn't work out for him. The autism held him back. In some way, he survived by not conforming. He had survived by observing and watching. He had survived by remaining true to himself and in dealing with life the only way he could understand.

I think the 'ideal' situation, if there is such a beast, is for a child to remain with family through the school years. After that, introduction into a group/waiver home setting could be realized. It didn't work out that way for us. I don't think it *could* have worked that way for us. His circumstances and ours were, and are, different. Shane's needs and priorities are unique unto himself. They are different than those of so many other people with developmental disabilities. So we're attempting to accomplish sort of a 'reverse' of the ideal situation.

In April of 2004, we took the plunge and began to serve Shane as a home setting. I had spent seventeen years in the service of other developmentally delayed persons. Now I could serve my own son, bringing what I had observed and learned with me. Shane's friend, one of his direct care attendants of several years, came with us. L.G. had doubts about the new and different program but took a deep breath and plunged in.

I continued to live at my residence thirty miles from Shane. However, I was at Shane's house more often than not as we started the programming. It wasn't easy. The years of being away from me had conditioned Shane to rethink my role in his life. I was there to visit, to take him on rides and out for treats. My actually living with him no longer existed in his realm. We spent countless afternoons of him attempting to get me to go home. He would chase/walk me around the car in the garage for hours. He screamed at me. The ONLY time Shane has attempted to use an item to strike out at someone was when he threw a fork at me. Shane and I collectively decided that perhaps we didn't even like each other. I began to wonder what we'd gotten in to.

He was adamant about my not sleeping at his house. When monitoring his care and when I simply had to be in his home early in the morning, I would have to sleep in my car. If he happened to sleep that night, I could sneak in and talk to staff. Otherwise, I had to spend the night in my car parked out of the driveway. We certainly were off to a good start!

I returned to my residence thirty miles one-way at least daily. There were the cats to be fed and I loved seeing my friend/dog, Dylan. Dylan and the cats always greeted me with affection. They always forgave me for the increase in my absence and time away from them. It took several weeks, but Shane did adjust to my being back in his life on more of a full-time basis. His acceptance came gradually at first, but soon he began to smile more. It appeared he had suspiciously accepted being a family again. Soon it appeared he once again enjoyed the stability and predictability of my presence.

I had returned to my residence and was having my car serviced at a local station when I received L.G.'s telephone call. They were in the emergency room. Shane had experienced a grand mal seizure. He was cyanotic, with no breath. His face had turned an ashen blue-grey as L.G. performed CPR. He was now resting easily and the physician assured me they would monitor him closely. My car was suspended on the garage hoist and I couldn't get to him. Hours later I arrived at the hospital. Shane was resting comfortably and soon we were to return home. The fear of being long distance away from my son remains with me.

In the days that followed his physician adjusted Shane's medications slightly. We watched him closely. Following the seizure, his agility and balance abilities decreased slightly again. I was convinced this had not been his first grand mal. I will always believe there were other seizures, undetected by staff who had not been observant, or perhaps not even present. That would explain why we had already noted a previous loss in his gait and balance.

Three months later Shane, Miles and I were sitting in Shane's living room. Shane was in his recliner, toying with a prized shoestring and laughing. The next instant he was in full seizure. Again he rapidly became cyanotic. Miles pulled his brother to the floor and started CPR while I tried to get a call through to 911. Shane was taken to the hospital for tests, and then released. He slept for seventeen hours. Again, his medications were 'tweaked' and increased to avert another grand mal seizure.

Life returned to 'normal', whatever that was or is. Shane had adjusted to the minor loss of balance and gait and was doing well. We were having fewer periods of aggression and self-abuse but the intensity was still high level. The medication adjustments appeared to stabilize his condition.

We made a second attempt of utilizing a communication board. Even though we introduced the newer and improved models of communication devices, he was not receptive to any he tried. The company had discontinued the model he had used in the beginning. One of the drawbacks was his compulsion to depress one key and simply not pay attention to what he was doing. The newer, advanced models didn't offer the ticker tape printouts and he didn't like the change. Our window of opportunity was closed.

One morning I was about 30 minutes driving time away from his house when I received another infamous emergency call from staff. Shane was in the hospital emergency room. His ear had been severed. By the time I arrived at the hospital, L.G, fire department personnel and hospital personnel were attempting to hold him in a prone position on the table. He had been highly sedated but in true Shane fashion had managed to fight off the effects of the medications. He was terrified and screaming. Everyone took turns holding him down, attempting to hold his ear close to his head while verbally attempting to calm him. His ear was held to his head with only a half-inch of cartilage. Because he had eaten some potato chips prior to the accident, surgery had to be postponed for several hours. It wasn't until we gave him a mirror so he could actually see what had happened to him that he calmed a bit. It proved to be a *very* long wait until the surgeons could repair the damage.

An aquarium had been in the corner of his living room as a statement of emphasis on relaxation techniques in his home. Occasionally he would watch the fish swimming and appeared to enjoy the serenity and sound of the circulating water. We had placed an ottoman in front of the aquarium area to deter him from going too close to the glass. The ottoman had been moved when staff vacuumed the room. I don't know if Shane was attempting to replace the ottoman to its proper place or if he just happened to be in the wrong place at the wrong time. He had fallen into the tank, breaking the glass and, thus, severing his ear. That was the end of having an aquarium in Shane's domain.

In the spring of 2005, we began our search for a home. We had only rented until then. Rentals have their drawbacks. They didn't allow dogs and I was anxious for Dylan to join us. We needed a house we could paint, decorate and personalize. We needed a home. It was going to be a permanent home for Shane and he seemed to be pleased with the prospects.

I did not and do not want to live with Shane. Constant exposure to his high energy profile can strip any person in the vicinity of their own energies. His erratic sleep habits and sporadic screaming/yelling at any hour of the day or night can make sleep for others impossible. Shane also has an uncanny instinct to 'know' what may be of importance to a person and he will quite intentionally target such objects for breakage. I do not value material things over my relationship with Shane. However, I would still cringe if he targeted some of the family items I've managed to salvage through the years.

In addition, I believe it is important for Shane to keep a certain level of independence. I had chosen to be of service to him in these latter years. I do believe, however, he needs to be somewhat weaned from my constant presence. His apartment need to be *his* very own personalized space. I need to live separately. Dually, I needed to be in close proximity, to monitor his services and assure his safety. The answer appeared to lie in our obtaining a duplex. Separate addresses. Separate residences. We began our search. We viewed some real rat-trap residences before our realtor found something that was clean, in a nice neighborhood, and affordable.

We moved into our new homes in June of 2005. Moving into a new neighborhood can always be an adventure for someone with developmental disabilities. One never knows the attitude or prejudices of the people who already live there. From my experience of working in the field, I was aware that many petitions have been signed in attempts to keep 'those people' out of their neighborhood. I think they must surely watch too many horror films. Their attitude toward the handicapped population is appalling and disheartening but it does exist.

Shane moved into his new home which is the lower level of the duplex first. While we were relocating his furniture and belongings, a lady came to the fence which separated our backyards. She greeted me warmly. I took a deep breathe and plunged into who we were and what we were all about. I told her she would probably hear screaming or yelling from Shane's home periodically at any given time, night or day. Sometimes there are screams of torment and anger. At other times, loud manic laughter is prevalent. It depends on what phase, or cycle he is experiencing. There are many moods and multiple phases affecting him and they are apt to change rapidly. I told her my son would be 'coming and going' for car rides at all hours of the day or night because he had no control over his sleep pattern and does not adhere to any day/night routine. I told her our lights were on 24 hours a day and it was an extremely busy household. I told her she had an adult with autism as a neighbor.

To my relief and delight, she stated that she didn't care what we did, as long as we liked living there. Linda is a kind hearted and wonderfully honest (tell it like it is) person who is cheerful and fun to be around. She exudes warmth and a marvelous sense of humor; she is our friend.

Other neighbors have also been friendly. They are aware of our situation. Some have experienced their own personal tragedies and accept what we are attempting to accomplish.

Several weeks after Shane was settled into his new home, I was able to move into my upstairs domain. The first moving trip brought Dylan to my home. I had an entire three-bedroom residence to move into a smaller area. We still have unpacked boxes in the garage and one day I may just pitch them, unopened. But as I become older, down-sizing is a good thing! Moving gives us the opportunity and reason to shed the vast accumulation of worthless and trivial 'stuff' we probably didn't need in the first place.

Had anyone told me, when he was a little guy sprinting around the house, that Shane would eventually require a wheelchair for outings, I would have thought they were crazy. The neurological decline has taken its toll. Two years ago his neurologist suggested we attend physical therapy sessions to strengthen his legs, and attempt to regain some of gait and balance difficulties. Shane appeared eager to attend the session, allowed the therapist to aid him in performing the exercises (perfectly!) and listened as she told him he would have to practice the exercises at home.

For the first four or five days, he was religious in the regime. But he wasn't seeing progress. By the end of the first week, he was doing fewer repetitions and, by the third week, refused to perform the exercises at all. I believe (again, seeing through his eyes) that he really thought the exercises would work their miracle. When he didn't see results, he abandoned the project. Period. Long-term projects and promises aren't in his patience zone. It marked another disappointment in his life.

He was angry and frustrated when the wheelchair was first introduced, but his good nature came through and he did accept his fate. He understands the use of the wheelchair opens his world to shopping at his favorite stores and just getting to the car for rides. Most of the larger stores supply their own wheelchairs. I wouldn't venture to instruct Shane in use of the electric ones, but there is usually a manual chair available. It saves us from constantly stuffing his chair into a car trunk. I smile when visualizing Shane driving wildly up and down the grocery aisles in an electric wheelchair. I know he'd think it was great fun, but woe to the other shoppers.

With security cameras installed in Shane's domain, I am able to monitor at will. It is a valuable tool to monitor Shane and his direct care personnel. It is an excellent tool to utilize when new staff may be in need of further training or clarification of house rules. With Shane's declined gait and balance, I can constantly be aware of any falls that may occur. Currently we have exceptionally good, seasoned personnel and I do not feel a need to constantly monitor their activities. I would sincerely advise a security system for anyone who has direct care staff working with their person. It is a safeguard for your person as well as for your home.

Shane creates his own programming. There are required goals which need to be addressed. The documented goals range from staff encouraging him to clean his room, aid in food preparation and the usual daily or weekly activities and areas which will aid him in becoming more independent. But for the most part, he runs the show. There will be no more attempts to force the proverbial square peg into the round hole. It has allowed Shane some control over his life. He can live life on

HIS time/sleep schedule and not adhere to the hours of outside programming.

He cannot be forced into having a roommate. He would cause serious physical and mental harm to both the attempted housemate, as well as to himself. He cannot tolerate day programming with other consumers. Day programming and workshops are activities he has rebelled against most of his life. They simply do not work for him.

I have evaluated the changes he has undergone since home services. He is more relaxed and smiles more. His vocabulary and willingness to share it has increased. He realizes home, security, and safety. He has choice. He is no longer pushed, coaxed, prodded into going to programming which makes no sense to him. We can accommodate his inability to deal with these situations. His sleep habits are respected, regardless of the hour, day and night. He is allowed to take life at a comfortable pace while being constantly aided and supported. He has learned better self-control when overwrought or over stimulated. We still have 'those' times when he reaches that point of return. Still, the frequency of spinning totally out of control in anger and frustration has decreased.

Although Shane has more control over his environment, he doesn't always get what he wants. Quite frequently he looks at me and emphasizes "grocery, grocery". If grocery shopping isn't on the day's agenda, I can tell him that we aren't going to the grocery today. We will go Tuesday. I attempt to be very specific about when he can go to the different stores. At times it appears he is pleased with himself simply because he has been able to express the word, grocery. We still have many days and many cycles when he is not able to express his thoughts into a word or phrase.

We've learned to monitor his demeanor. If he just doesn't appear to feel well or is grimacing, we take the lead in attempts to discover his needs. We might have to ask him several times if he needs headache medicine. If he does, he will repeat the "headache medicine". If he doesn't and the word "No" isn't available to him, he will fall back on the old technique of looking away and ignoring us.

We no longer offer foods (or anything) without some validation from him as to whether he actually wants it or not. We have learned not to assume. He may request tuna for six days in a row, but then may not want it for six months. Except for cheese, his food preferences vary and it is difficult to 'buy ahead' to accommodate his pantry or refrigerator. I believe it was the week I had to throw away three cartons of 'turned' cottage cheese that I finally stopped assuming I could stock food in advance just because he liked it last week. Stocking up because items may currently be on sale doesn't work well for us unless it is something with a lengthy shelf life.

I have been reflecting how very much he has changed over the past three years. Miles says Shane just seems happier. L.G has been with him for six years, through many of our traumatic experiences. I asked him how he would summarize the positive change in Shane.

With regards to how much Shane has changed since entering a personalized program, L.G. states: "The big full-face smile on Shane's face was unexpected as he said, 'just joking around.'. I can remember wondering if I would ever see him smile. Today he was clearly proud of himself. The moment caused me to reflect on six years ago when I was introduced to Shane. I recall wondering if this angry, frightened and insecure young man would ever enjoy life. He was considered to be non-verbal, communicating mostly by tantrums or worse. He had a sad, fearful look in his eyes not quite hiding the years of torment of living in a state developmental center. A look just a few weeks [of being released to an agency] could not erase." "Shane now trusts people who assist him in his daily activities. He is visibly happy and more secure. Tantrums have gone from nearly constant to occasional. Shane still has self-abusive behaviors and sometimes becomes physically aggressive when frustrated. However these times now are a few minutes in duration, instead of continuing for hours." "The difference in Shane's demeanor and attitude are staggering since moving to a family setting. He is still extremely ornery, but now it's more to surprise or tease than to be hateful or destructive. The bright sparkle-in-his-eyes-smile says it all. [It is] priceless." [L.G.H.]

L.G. is one of the 'good guys'; he has Shane's trust and friendship. At no time have I had doubted his commitment to Shane. He forgives me for my sporadic ramblings and ravings about nothing in particular and I forgive him for his occasional attempts to sneak recyclable items into the trash.

One mid-morning I was sitting on his sofa when Shane came over to sit by me. He took my and looked directly into my eyes. This, in itself, was highly unusual. But then he said, "I want to die." I talked calmly to him, telling him that it just wasn't his time to die yet. I told him I understood. The moment was very brief and it was over in a moment. It was a chilling look into his thoughts. It gave me a new understanding for the depths of his anguish and the weariness of his soul.

We scheduled a visit with his psychiatrist. I had called ahead so the psychiatrist would be aware of the incident without talking about it in front of Shane. He asked Shane if he was ever sad. Shane repeated, "sad". An anti-depressant was added to his medications. He remains on this medication although we have had the dose reduced due to his weight gain.

Some of his major fears have dissipated. He had been terrified of dogs for his entire life. He could tolerate cats, but upon seeing a dog, he would scale his caregiver's body until he was almost setting on their head. When I moved Dylan into my apartment, I began introducing Dylan as we would 'pass through' Shane's kitchen. Exposure was limited at first. As Shane began to show tolerance, Dylan was allowed to spend short periods of time in Shane's home. In two years' time, he not only 'tolerated' Dylan, but would watch his antics and laugh. After 30 years of being afraid of dogs, he learned to actually like and accept this gentle dog.

Dylan was a very special companion to me. He was one of the gentlest souls I have ever had the pleasure of knowing. He was part Beagle and part whatever. He would nose the trail of a rabbit or chipmunk in the backyard, but could pass within three feet of them, look them in the eye, and keep walking. He was the 'best ever' therapy dog for Shane. Dylan was my confidante, friend, and companion. When my shift was over, Dyl and I would take off to car ride and spend time together.

In the first week of May, Dylan suffered a stroke. He was fourteen years old. At first it appeared he may recover. He did not. By the end of May, he was weak and paralyzed. He could barely drink water as I held his head close to his dish. I anguished over making the decision to aid in putting an end to his suffering. I called my friend who works with the Humane Society. It was Memorial Day weekend, but she agreed to meet us. She was ever so kind and understanding as I stayed with Dylan during the euthanasia process. I could only offer him love and comfort as he crossed over. We had lost a valuable family member.

In June of 2007, I gave thought to accrediting our own company with State. That would mean we would be a service provider business. Currently, the company we are subcontracted under handles the billing process. By becoming accredited and assuming all of the necessary roles, it would allow additional funds for our budget, which we could funnel into Shane's needs.

Being reasonably ambitious and work-oriented, I have been comfortable in working both full-time and part-time employment simultaneously during my most of my adulthood. There's always a financial need commanding additional funds. With Shane, it is usually in the form of replacing breakage. We are in need of a new mattress and box spring set at least every four months. Recliners have a lifespan of (perhaps) one year. Even with staff vigilance and attentiveness to cleaning the intentional staining on Shane's bedroom carpet, our carpet cleaner shows signs of an impending demise. Due to his intentional urination and defecation in his room, we have a need to replace his carpeting with linoleum. I have attempted to 'save' the carpeted area because it provides cushion in case he should fall, or if he bangs his head against the floor. He may balk at the major change in his living quarters, but it appears linoleum is the answer to maintaining a sanitary environment. For some unknown reason, we also manage to 'go through' the life expectancy of at least three vacuum sweepers a year. Household cleaning is a major yearly expense.

Some families do not fair as well with the financial strains of keeping up with maintenance. Breakage in their domain might extend to windows, glass patio doors and other costly items. We are indeed fortunate. We only need to keep a large container of all-purpose joint compound available to patch holes in the drywall. During allergy season, Shane will still occasionally head-butt into drywall. Wall maintenance needs now are usually due to his intense and accelerated rocking in his recliner.

Miles and I attended a State meeting for potential service providers. Although they were informative and friendly, the process seemed overwhelming. We had 30 days in which to provide everything from proof of being a company to policies/procedures to required documentation on almost every aspect of one's life. During the accreditation process, I felt inept and helpless. We needed the expertise of a lawyer, a CPA, and the person we would subcontract with to prepare the policy and procedures. It would be equivalent of our becoming an agency ourselves. It would mean immersing in business on a 100% basis. The next thirty days were frantic and time consuming.

I kept searching for signs that this was something we were 'meant to do'. But I kept hitting snags. Perhaps that *was* the sign. Murphy's Law prevailed at almost our every turn. The bottom line was that we were simply not in a good financial position to even consider becoming a provider service agency. It had been a wild and exhausting ride. I was disappointed in our failure to become accredited, but also felt relieved. Perhaps relieved is an understatement. For the first time in weeks I could breathe easier, turning my attentions back to the business of managing Shane's home.

Not all was lost. Out of our experience with the attempt to become accredited, we gained a very capable and experienced CPA. He has an adult sister who is developmentally delayed. He understands our situation very well, as well as the families of other people serving their family member. He's patient with me and good natured when I ask muddled questions. He lets me know what paperwork I need to send in…and when. He is aware the monthly and quarterly 'business' matters play a fourth role in the orchestration of home services.

First and foremost are the responsibilities, time constraints and immediate demands of care giving. Second, there are State regulations to comply with and daily/ monthly reports which command attention. It is the State and Federal funds which support our fragile population, which makes the paperwork an easier pill to swallow. The System is continually attempting to provide safe environments and optimum health care for our people.

In third place are the matters pertaining to direct care people which require an ongoing support system and attention to detail. As stated previously, 'business' matters are in fourth place. No matter the circumstances, as family members caring for our people, we must not allow for deviation in the order of our priorities.

Of course there's the fifth…and sixth categories of your personal life and all of the ta-dah that goes with that, *should the time and energy arise*. If you think you have all of your bases covered, something will arise to let you know differently.

During the month of June, we were aware Shane was undergoing another of his neurological 'spirals'. They usually are not stark and significant changes, but we who know him best can notice the differences. There are subtle and occasional 'palsied' tremors of his left side that usually occur during his sleep cycle. This is followed by days of obvious frustration at a very slight yet noticeable decline in his gait and balance. We are always supportive of Shane and his needs, but during these times extra attention is needed to observe the subtle changes. We are tolerant of his angry outbursts, knowing he is confused and experiencing added frustration with his loss of skills. During these times he is 'grumpier'. He tires more easily and requires more sleep.

Still, I admire his high level of courage. While most people would not perceive Shane to be a particularly tolerant person, we who know him best realize what a brave individual he actually is. He is a very strong and persevering individual.

In July, I was still grieving the loss of Dylan. Although I could never replace him, I knew it was time to add a new friend to my life. Miles, Shane, and I stopped at a farmhouse with a sign in the yard advertising 'puppies for sale'. Shane watched with interest as I selected a puppy from the four remaining liter mates. I don't think we select puppies, kittens, or friends. I believe they select us. Forty dollars later, 'Mike' was sitting in Miles's lap as we drove home. He is mixed breed of black Labrador retriever (mother) and Australian blue heeler cattle dog (father dog's breed was unknown until much later). Mike is highly intelligent, rapidly learning new commands and 'tricks'. But living in close quarters with a herding dog is worth a chapter in itself.

Shane appears to be amused with the puppy's antics. He is actually very tolerant with Mike and is usually laughing as he retrieves some of his property the puppy has stolen from his room. Occasionally I have observed him sneaking tid-bits and left over food from his plate to Mike. Shane has grown so very much from being the fearful young man who was terrified of dogs.

To the dismay of my cats, Mike enjoys showing off his inherent herding skills. Eschigoya Cat wouldn't have anything to do with me for the first three days after Mike moved into my apartment. Things have settled down somewhat since then, but I know it will be a very long time before Mike grows out of 'puppyhood'. While he flies around my apartment with wild puppy abandon between our training session times, he is quite different with Shane. During my hours of direct care, I can bring Mike to Shane's domain. Mike is reserved and quiet, allowing me to focus my attentions on Shane's needs. He 'read' Shane in a short time period and is respectful, of Shane's space and moods.

I had to question my sanity at taking on the added responsibility of a puppy. My plate was already full. Still, I knew the answer lay in my need for reciprocated love. Although I believe Shane is capable of loving, he does not display validation of his affections, save for the 'trained' hugs. Being the parent of an autistic individual can be a very lonely position.

The animals I have had the pleasure of knowing do give freely of their devotion and affection. I simply needed a companion to drive with, to interact with, and to share the fun times with. The slobbery puppy kisses and adoring brown eyes are an added bonus. Michael is hard-headed and has a mind of his own, which means he is very much like everyone else in our domain. He fits in. As he matures, the positive trait of loyalty emerges. He is bonded to and is protective of Shane and his circle of support. He has also formed a friendship with the cats, which was a great surprise.

The events of our 2007 summer forced me to reevaluate my life. The universe truly does work in strange, mysterious and wondrous ways, as always. There are those parents (and some professional people in the field) who thrive on devoting their entire life to autism. I found myself needing more. I was drowning in my self-inflicted saturation of eating, breathing, and living autism every waking moment. It was simply a matter of overkill. I was drained and depleted of my energies, becoming ineffective in all areas of my life.

I had been working part time as quality assurance for almost a year, being subcontracted to work with other families in our area who were also serving their people within home settings. There were meetings to be attended and paperwork in the individual homes to check, but there was also a lot that I could perform from home. The cell phone could also be utilized as Shane and I went for our numerous and sometimes constant car outings.

Working as direct care with Shane six days a week allows him the stability of a predictable routine. I attempt to keep my 'shift' to six hours a day. But I choose to frequently see him at intervals throughout the evening and am on call for back up support twenty-four hours a day. I need to be close by should he seizure or go into a behavior that would require having two staff with him. We have not had to utilize a PRN for additional sedation in over two years now. But I would have to be present should the need arise.

In addition, I get to be the person who keeps up with the laundry, lawn and property maintenance and all of those other fun duties we parents do in our spare time to maintain a household. There are the administrative duties of managing his household. This is inclusive of the responsibility of State required paperwork, banking, and paying the independent contractors who are Shane's direct care staff. Just when you believe you have one dragon subdued, another rears its head.

There was also the ongoing concern of watching my mother deteriorate, both physically and mentally. When Shane was a little guy, one of his favorite people was Grandma. He was her only grandson for four years and she adored him. Shane could do no wrong, in her eyes. She loved him dearly. She could not understand autism, even though I supplied her with every book available. She could not understand that his inability to communicate had absolutely nothing to do with his intelligence. She doted on him and always refused to believe his condition might be permanent. She was, however, supportive of me when I made the decision to institutionalize him. It must have been difficult for her to watch the internal struggle I dealt with. It isn't until we become a parent that we can truly and finally understand our own.

My mother has been in a nursing home for the past ten years. Unable to care for herself, she spends much of her time sleeping. Emotionally she appears to recognize me but is confused much of the time. Shane remembers Grandma vividly and says "Grandma" periodically. There has been only one attempt to take Shane to visit her in the past year. When we arrived at her room, he grasped her hand and tried to pull her from her bed. When she couldn't respond, he busied himself with riffling through her bedside stand looking for toothpaste. When he couldn't find his favorite brand, he was ready to leave. Although Shane appeared to enjoy the visit, it confused and upset Mother.

Now I visit Mother solo when I can. Under hospice care for failure to thrive, she sleeps a lot. There are days when she recognizes and clings to me. During other visits, she may confuse me for someone else. Dementia is taking its toll. My time constraints dictate only one or two visits with her per week. If she could, she would understand my not being able to see her more often. For so many years she was dedicated to me. She would understand my commitment and responsibilities to my son.

I was once again drained emotionally, mentally, and physically. We need to know ourselves. That includes knowledge of our limitations as well as our strengths. Just realizing our weaknesses can steer us into areas of strength. I learned not to make decisions while in the grieving process. I had also recently quit smoking. One of the stupidest things I did at the age of 17 was to start smoking. A second stupid thing I did was quit. For me, it was a coping mechanism. Besides, I feel everyone needs at least one vice.

It was also during this time that clumsiness, or perhaps divine providence, caused me to walk directly into a bicycle hanging from the garage ceiling. I hit it hard enough to dislocate it from it's secured ceiling hooks. I realized several days later that I had a concussion with all of the lovely symptoms. After the light-headedness, nausea and vision blurring cleared, I remained a bit woozy. For weeks I found myself forgetting what I was saying in mid-sentence. The incident literally knocked some sense into my head. What had I been thinking for the past months?

I thrive on people, nature, spiritual issues and the arts. My interests do not lie in the realm of business/corporate matters. Because my interests and talents are not inclusive of these areas, I am unable, or choose not to give them the time and attention necessary to succeed. In essence, I am not a businesswoman. The very idea of spending more, not less time at the computer or on the cell phone discussing business matters drives me over my boundaries. I had lost sight of the fact that one person can only accomplish so much with any expertise whatsoever. It is unwise to go into deep waters if you can't swim. Or if you simply don't want to swim.

Life is simply a matter of choosing priorities and not spreading one's self too thin across too many areas. It appears that happens all too frequently in today's society. I had not only forgotten to smell the proverbial roses. I had lost sight of the entire garden.

The physical signs of extreme stress were present. I lived in a constant 'fight or flight' response. At first I ignored the symptoms, chalking everything up to the advancing years and getting older. Then there were the all too often memory lapses, continuous upper respiratory infections, weight loss and general weakness. I had entered into a hazardous zone. One never knows if the health or the psyche will break first.

Caregivers often lose sight of their own needs. Many people in the nursing profession are prime examples. Two good friends, Angie and Elaine, have discussed this matter with me on several occasions. Both of these ladies wear the title of R.N.

Caregivers who truly care about the people they come into contact with are especially vulnerable. I often think of the thousands of wives or husbands who care for an aging spouse with little to no regard for their own health. I also take note of the stress many other stay-at-home mothers experience.

My friend Carolyn used to emphasis to me that you could not take care of someone else until you could take care of yourself. Ignoring one's own self is a common trait of caregivers. There are frequent evenings when I suddenly realize I haven't taken the time to even eat that day. There were many days I would see my reflection in a store window or display and realize I looked the same as when I had crawled out of bed that morning. Makeup and attention to detail was pursued only one day a week when I would be scheduled with massage therapy appointments or the once-in-a-blue-moon sushi and wine dinner with an old and valued friend.

I could accept my hair graduating from the auburn brown it had been to a very stark white. I could cope with the usual signs of aging. But with that considered, I was unable to recognize the person I had become. As the inevitable and nagging signs of aging begin to plague me, I attempt to 'do better'. It takes care and energy to choreograph our dance through life. Carolyn's words ring in my ears on an almost daily basis.

I recall the words of another mother who was struggling with her son's autism and his programming. She felt families of autistic individuals should have a written contract that made them immune to the frustrations of ordinary, everyday life. We shouldn't be required to also deal with leaky water pipes, lousy finances and people who do not pay what they owe to you, inconsiderate people at the grocery store, or drivers who cut you off in traffic. She is the lady who said she wanted to reincarnate in the next life as a rock.

There are so many people of various maladies who require complete care. They rely totally on the support of other souls. It is very easy for the caregiver to give so completely that they lose sight of their own lives, forgetting that they, too, are an entity. There is nothing wrong with taking care of other people, as long as the caregiver does not lose sight of their own health and interests. Martyrdom isn't all its cracked up to be. For whatever path an individual chooses, they should remember that they can give care and attention to others and simultaneously personalize their own existence.

We have not had a tragic life. There are so many people in our world, past and present, who have known heartache, insurmountable pains and hardships that I will never realize. What had brought me physical and mental exhaustion was that the situation was and is constant. I believe the word, relentless would best sum up the situation. Yes, 'relentless' says it all.

In the beginning of that Fall, I cut back on the hours I was spending with my quality assurance work. Miles is a qualified QMRP and could attend many of the meetings held in the family homes, which would allow for my cut back in scheduling. I could attend a few meetings and attend to the telephone calls and paperwork. The company I am subcontracted with has good communication and organizational skills, which also makes life a bit easier.

Giving up personal face-to-face contact with some of the families I had worked for and with would be difficult. Each family has their own unique situation and coping skills. I am in constant awe of the courage and creativity of the families we have had the pleasure of meeting. Some of those people will always be an important and valued addition to my life.

I could now focus my attentions more intently on Shane. The lasting effects of each spiral loss are extremely difficult for him. He is angry and frustrated over the consistent loss of his gross motor skills. He strikes out often. He is weary and requires extra support. It is for my benefit as much as it is for him. Sometimes I catch myself peeking in on him as he sleeps, to make sure he is breathing alright and resting well. It is just as I did so many, many years ago. Some things never change.

In order to increase our cash flow, I fell back on working very part-time as a massage therapist once again. A very nice young lady I had worked with previously had recently opened a spa. She is spiritual, innovative and progressive, allowing for the use of essential oils during facials and massage work. To be able to work with clients to alleviate pain and stress is immensely rewarding. Most of my clientele come for bodywork on a regular basis. Friendships are formed and it gives me a sense of communal belonging as opposed to the isolation of Shane's home. Massage therapy is physically demanding. However, I am able to schedule only one day a week with a limited number of clientele. A spa can be an oasis of relaxation. The music, the services, the ambience are all tuned to reduce stress. For relieving stress, it appears the therapies offered benefit the therapist as well as the client. For me, it is also several hours out of my usually mundane yet overwhelming routine.

Many years ago, when I first went into the field of massage therapy, I was unaware that some people would offer a raised eyebrow and a snicker when you tell them you are a therapist. To these people, I can only say that it's time to grow up and get over it. The shady 'massage parlors' are simply not a part of a true therapist's vocabulary. Massage therapy is designed to benefit not only the muscular and nervous systems, but also the digestive, circulatory, respiratory, lymph and integumentary (skin) stems. It is a major asset for health and stress relief.

Many persons with autism do not care for, or cannot accept massage due to an overload it may place on their sensory systems. When addressing the population of persons with other mental challenges, the therapist must be aware and cautious. The emotional and psychological release of massage can be overwhelming for some people, particularly those in middle age. Some of these people have lived a life of being shunned and isolated with little to no close physical contact from another human being.

It was good to return to the field of massage therapy. It was almost like greeting a beloved friend who had been absent for too, too long! This is of importance only because it conveys a message. We need activities and people in our lives that make and allow us to smile. When we are able to connect with happiness, we can pass it to those around us. When we are at peace with ourselves, we can convey that message of serenity to those around us, to those who sincerely benefit.

There is now more time to pursue my own interests. I attempt to stay close to Shane's home in case I am needed. But I also am involved with the personal activities that bring me joy. There's always gardening to be done although that becomes boring and even difficult by the time the mid-summer heats sets in. There is a bit of time to read and stay informed about the latest archaeological discoveries. Visiting with friends is always a welcomed activity. Sitting in the quiet of a nature setting away from the confusion of the world brings peace.

My father had shared his love of nature with me at a very early age. He taught me to observe and respect what the environment offered. He was a gentle, quiet, and intensely intelligent man. He left this plane all too soon, crossing over the week prior to my high school graduation. With each of my pregnancies, I planned how I would pass on to my children what my father had taught me. I once saw a church signboard which stated, 'How do you make God laugh? Tell him your plans for the future'.

Mike and I often go for car rides, stopping at a drive-thru for an iced tea and small bowl of water (respectively). While driving, we listen to a wide variety of music. Tom Waits, Eric Clapton, Bessie Smith and Son House are just a few of the artists who make me smile. Kitaro allows my mind and soul to soar. Mike seems to accept a wide array of music styles. He is a grand companion. He takes me for brisk walks. Sometimes we sit very quietly and just enjoy all that life has to offer.

It is very easy to give advice to others. It is also easy to ignore good advice yourself. With that in mind, I would also advise other parents to heed Carolyn's words. Common sense reigns supreme. Eat sensibly. Sleep soundly. Take time to consult with your physician if the need arises. Laugh a lot and laugh frequently. Respect yourself. Have faith in your abilities. Embrace your friendships. Recognize and cultivate your spirituality. Take time to smell the roses. Talk to people face-to-face, openly and honestly. Demand your right to live simplistically in our complex world.

Part II

The Destination
A Portrait of Shane

Shane is now 32 years of age. From the 'hyperactivity of the early years', he has mellowed. His general demeanor is subdued from the uncontrollable toddler and child we knew so many years ago. Although he can still be combative, the episodes have become fewer, and more manageable. Perhaps this is due to a well-orchestrated medication regime and to his maturation. Ironically, the neurological decline which causes him to move slowly also allows us to 'keep up with him'.

The diagnosis, to date, includes autism, moderate mental retardation (?), impulse control disorder and obsessive/ compulsive disorder; he is also bi-polar. Shane can be helpful, amiable, interactive and absolutely delightful to be with. He can also be extremely aggressive both to those around him and, mainly, to himself (self injurious behaviors, or SIBs). To ensure his safety, and to monitor his health needs on an ongoing basis, he requires at least one direct care person to be with him at almost all times. He does have time for himself when he is in his room as this is his safe haven. He utilizes the space for privacy, play and for self-calming.

After many years of attempting to see the world through his eyes, I can accept and understand his autism. Only someone afflicted with autism truly knows the inner turmoil, but we who live *beside* the autism do attain some degree of insight and understanding. I have learned to 'roll with the tide' when it comes to his bi-polarity.

The obsessive/compulsive disorder is frustrating for all of us. When he is feeling distressed, he will obsess on a particular item or activity relentlessly. Usually, he requests mouthwash repeatedly until someone complies with his request. After receiving the mouthwash, he delights not in using it, but in dumping the bottle's contents down the drain. After he has accomplished his mission of 'receive and destroy', he is usually in a very good mood. The obsessive phase may last for hours until he either gets/finds what he wants or tires and sleeps. The phase may also abruptly end with a period of severe SIBs, usually hitting himself in the face, screaming loudly and kicking his own legs and then finally falling asleep. He can be extremely intense and driven.

It is his impulse control disorder that I feel is the most distressing. One minute we are having a relatively good day and are planning a car ride or shopping trip that he would enjoy. The next minute our plans are cancelled or postponed because he could not resist the sudden urge to pour a glass of water onto the floor, intentionally defecate on the floor, or do something equally irritating. After the fact, he is usually angry with himself and perhaps also confused by the lack of self-control.

During our earlier years, I would become irritated when people would tell my son that he *knew* better and therefore he *could do* 'better'. It seemed as though it was like telling a person with no legs that they should be able to walk in a normal fashion. As much as he tried (and there were times he tried very hard), it just wasn't good enough. If a person is born with no legs, it is likely that person will find their own way to get about and around in the world. That person may do very well on their life path, but the hard fact is that they will not walk in the same manner as the person with two healthy legs. By the same reasoning, a person with the life-long condition of autism may not get around in the world in the same manner as the person who is not afflicted. They will take avenues and roads in life that are of comfort to them. By constantly telling a person they could 'do' better, the implications are that they simply aren't living up to the expectations of those closest to them.

It is mandatory we encourage a person to do all they are capable of doing and assist in presenting new and challenging windows of opportunity for growth. However we must be extremely mindful of how we verbalize and present our support to that person. People with autism tend to be very literal. Too often the message sent in not-so-subtle ways is, "You're not quite what I expected. Your actions not acceptable or good enough (you're not good enough). The mannerisms you find comfort in are not acceptable. You don't fit in. You must become like the rest of us."

Instead, the message spoken and felt might best be expressed as "I love you very much. You are a good person. If and when you would like help with anything, I am here for you and I will support you". It's all about trust and self-esteem.

It is also about the Golden Rule. If I had autism and could not stop or control sporadic episodes of bizarre or self-injurious behaviors, I doubt I'd make much progress if I were continually told I was not trying hard enough. After awhile, I might stop trying altogether. Being stubborn by nature, I would probably retreat further into a world that was comfortable and not quite as demanding as a world I didn't understand anyway.

We are all different. We are all important in the tapestry of life. It is good that each of us can realize someone likes and accepts us *for who we are*. Acceptance is comforting and nurturing. Acceptance is the honey in a world full of vinegar.

For the past eight years, we have attended annual appointments at a genetic counseling center. The physician overseeing Shane's case is knowledgeable, experienced and thorough. Shane has undergone an array of tests to determine if any particular syndrome is present and if there would be any treatments which might be beneficial for him. If there were detectable and easy answers to my son's condition, I am confident the genetics physician would have found them in the first tests. However, the testing has failed to produce any conclusive evidence. The etiology of his condition is unknown. Having once been determined to find out the cause of my son's difficulties, I can honestly say it doesn't seem as important any more. Still, we will continue to pursue any leads on new and innovative testing that might be performed. I just doubt if it would make a difference at this stage of his life. There is a point in life when one simply accepts life for what it is.

Shane's sleep habits are erratic and his hours of sleep vary on a daily basis. Some of the factors that effect his demeanor are headaches (frontal lobe or sinuses, usually), Spring and Fall allergies, fluctuation of his depakote levels (Depakote, or Valproic Acid is utilized to prevent seizure activity), having to "wait" anywhere (not good at taking turns or waiting in physician offices), over stimulation in crowded stores, changes in the people around him (losing a staff or if staff switch 'shifts').

Variance in barometric pressure also greatly affects his demeanor. He struggles to be 'pleasant' when there are storm fronts and weather changes in the area. In addition, the frustration of being trapped within himself and the intense frustration of attempting to 'deal with' his neurological decline affects his behaviors. He has a lot to deal with.

He will repeat the phrase, "E-yow-wo" when 'something' is wrong. I sincerely believe these times denote he is experiencing an increase of brain sensations (light frontal lobe seizures?).

He also appears to be extremely sensitive to the moods of those people around him. He appears to 'tune in' on their present energies and absorb their demeanor into his own. Perhaps that is another reason for his distaste for crowds in the fact that it would simply be overkill of sensory issues.

Shane is at 'high risk' for an array of issues. They include home and community safety, vision, choking, mobility, medication side effects, elopement and his allergy to bee stings. Elopement isn't classified as high as it was when his mobility was less impeded. Since his gait and balance have undergone loss, I doubt that he would attempt to go too far from his home.

He remains on a high medication regime. It has been trial and error, but stability has been on his side now for several years. His physicians have fine tweaked and modified his medication regime. The goal is to stabilize the levels of his medications in his system throughout the day instead of having periods of 'highs and lows'. Instead of receiving higher doses of medications less often, he receives lower dosages at more frequent intervals. It is somewhat inconvenient with more frequent administration, but he has benefited significantly from the constant medication levels.

Last year Shane's psychiatrist suggested we put him on a 4,000 mg. daily dose of Omega3 Fish Oils. We began with four 1,000 mg. capsules, staggering the dose to accommodate his rapid metabolism. Because we saw no adverse effects, the dosage was increased to 5,000 mg., then 6,000 mg. daily. At a daily dose of 6,000 mg, we noticed he seemed to be grumpier and, for lack of a better term, mean. After decreasing the dose back to 5,000 mg., we noted his speech increased slightly. There was appropriateness to his word formation and a slight increase in the frequency of verbalization. At this writing, he remains on the 5,000 mg. per day dosage. It is also given at intervals throughout a twenty-four hour period due to his rapid rate of metabolism.

With regards to supplements, he also receives an acidophilus pearl, 200 mg. of Vitamin E and a gel cap multivitamin daily. Shane's psychiatrist is extremely knowledgeable with the recent studies in the field of autism. Recently we have added P-5-P (Pyridoxal-5-Phosphate). It is still too soon to note possible benefits, but to date we have been very pleased with the supplements he has recommended.

His weekly depakote readings are erratic and can often drop or raise by 10 to 25 points in a single week. This fluctuation is monitored closely by his neurologist on a weekly basis. Even taking dietary issues into consideration, the etiology of this fluctuation is unknown. Shane has become good friends with Sue, the technician at the blood lab. Before he comes in, she hides the small rubber band tourniquet used for most blood draws. After being restrained for many years in years gone-by, he has a hatred of anything that even resembles a restraint. Sue lets him choose two suckers after his draw. We both think she's great.

With two staff present, we can usually attend scheduled physician appointments and the blood lab, even if it means waking him up from sleep. All of his physicians know him well. He is only scheduled to be the first patient seen in the morning, or directly after lunchtime. Patience in having to wait his turn is certainly not one of his virtues. Foot stomping, screaming, and sporadic attempts to hit people in close proximity to his wheelchair tend to frighten the other patients present. I am sure they are equally alarmed by his loud vocalizations coming from the examination rooms when he has to wait too long to be seen by the physician.

I usually try to explain the situation when scheduling with new or less frequently seen physicians. If they choose to follow some unwritten office protocol and do it their way, all is not lost. If new receptionists ignore our attempts to inform them of the circumstances, it is usually rectified by the end of the first or second visit. It generally only takes that amount of time before they know to usher him into an examination room, away from the front office waiting room *upon arrival*. Most persons who are unfamiliar with severe autism and/or Shane Boldt are trainable after only a few attempts (tongue-in-cheek).

Still, during times of extreme emergency, he can be a model patient. I've observed him rallying to the occasion for an X-ray, stitches, or any array of other patient scenarios. Everything in his life hinges on the ever-present outside influences and the level of his inner turmoil. He is well aware of the cooperation required during office or hospital visits under more urgent conditions.

My son can be a major pistol, or an asset to anyone he knows. It all depends on his mood at the time. When 'all systems are go', a term I use when he is not effected by fluctuating blood level readings, seasonal allergies, or any of the previously mentioned factors, he is an absolute delight to be around. He valiantly strives to be pleasant and I've heard more once by store clerks who have dealt with him, that he is absolutely "adorable".

We have periods of time when he is able to be in touch with the environment around him. During those times he is happy, interactive and attentive. His speech usually comes more easily to him during those times and he enjoys his favorite activities. During these times, he appears to be genuinely content with himself and with life. He smiles, teases, and relates to the world in a friendly manner.

We also have hours and sometimes days of his inability to relate to his surroundings and environment. These days usually bring a fervent intensity to his self-aggression and self-abuse. His appetite decreases dramatically. He screams or yells undecipherable words and phrases continually. He paces or rocks feverishly in his recliner. He stares into space or at his hands as he waves them in the air. He does not 'hear' us or respond to any attempts to gain his attention. He is withdrawn into the abyss of autism. He may ram his head into the wall or onto the floor. When he does communicate during these times, he is demanding and angry. He is unreachable.

His demeanor may change rapidly, within minutes. It is though something clicks a switch 'on' and 'off'. With maturation, he has attained the ability to self-calm more easily. The situation requires a delicate balance of knowing when to intervene, offering support, and when to 'back off' to allow him to stabilize. Now that he is older, he may go to his room to play with blocks, sensory items, or simply lie down to compose.

Even his unpredictability has become more predictable over the years. Cycles of extreme self-injurious behaviors and aggression are usually proceeded by low guttural sounds and a total inability to relate to his surroundings. He becomes unreachable and we are unable to redirect his attentions. If low depakote levels are present he may 'throw' his head back repeatedly. During rare and especially hard times, he may walk rigidly, almost zombie-like, as he attempts to hit, bite, or scratch at his caregiver. His eyes 'change'. You can always tell what lies ahead by looking into his eyes.

When any adverse factors are present, his ability to deal with life dwindles. Intentional urination or defecation on the floor occurs frequently. It is a major goal, at this time, to consider replacing his bedroom carpeting with linoleum. That, however, would increase the chances of his falling on the wet surface. We haven't made a decision on the lesser of the two evils at this time. Less common but still of concern, is the intentional breakage of targeted items. Of course the self injurious behaviors and aggression to those around him increase during these times, also. It is our responsibility to determine the 'reason' for his discomfort. Searching for answers for the etiology of his demeanor is often like searching for the haystack's hidden needle.

Shane is at the mercy of the elements, and of the inner turmoil which plagues him. It is because of this side of his life that he was once banned from several grocery stores and one YMCA in our city. Customers tend to complain when someone is screaming, yelling and attempting to kick every baby stroller in sight. We haven't been asked to leave a store in several years now, so I'm chalking it up to progress made.

Even on a good day, the, checkout clerk may be greeted with "You have a nice day!" or the other mood, "You g__ dammit!". That would depend on his demeanor at the time, and on his sense of humor. In attempts to meet him halfway, I've bargained with him that "dammit" is O.K., but he really needs to leave God out of it.

Shane continues to delight in performing the negative acts which he knows will upset people. He knows, even when they are trying very hard not to show their frustration. After 32 years, he still enjoys the reaction. Occasionally I can observe a look of pride on his face when he has done something well, but it is best to 'downplay' these times. Praise doesn't generally work well with him. It is just as it was when he was the little guy who used to color pictures.

Christmas remains a difficult time for the family. It almost appears that Shane intentionally sabotages the holiday season. It is of very little interest for him, with the exception of presents and extra seasonal foods. It's almost as though he doesn't want anyone around him to be in an exceptionally 'happy' mood. The last decorated tree we had was two years ago. After about the fifth time he pulled it over while laughing hysterically, I boxed and sealed the decorations, permanently. We can get by with buffet style Thanksgiving and Christmas meals, but decorations must be kept to a minimum. Still, he appears to delight in trimmed trees at stores and decorated lawns during the season.

The only holiday Shane appears to enjoy is his birthday. He requests "cake candles" at intervals throughout the year and is delighted when his birthday approaches. It is one of the few times he doesn't mind extra people coming into his home. Everyone knows ahead of time to at least bring a beef stick or some other favorite item. He also allows for decorations during this time. The day is all for Shane and he rallies to the occasion.

I have heard people describe autism as the ultimate form of narcissism. I see no reason to disagree with them.

His long-term memory is excellent. Shane's ability to remember names of people he has not seen in decades astounds me. He is always pleased to see an old teacher or aide who had worked with him many years previously. Occasionally he will ask for 'Daddy', even though he has not seen him in over twenty years. Just 'Daddy' is reserved for his biological father. In later years, he would attach the name 'Daddy Jim' or 'Daddy Sam' to a staff if they were particularly protective of him. Somehow along the road, his friend and staff L.G. became 'Grandma L.G.'. It isn't an especially flattering title for a male staff. But Shane always adored his grandmother, so I suppose it's an extreme and high compliment to his good friend.

I do not believe his short-term memory fairs as well. Perhaps it is the words, and not the memory that fails him when asked where he was or what he ate only ten minutes ago.

Love is such a difficult term! If I look at it as unconditional trust, acceptance, familiarity and bonding, then I am assured my son loves me. He gravitates to those people who genuinely care for him. Does he actually *feel* love for me – or anyone? In my heart and soul, I would like to believe so. When he looks at me directly and smiles serenely I feel he is expressing his inner emotions.

However, heartfelt affection from Shane is, for the most part, non-existent. I have noted, in the past three decades, perhaps 3 or 4 times when he has come to me, on his own, and offered any degree of affection, or of bonding *when he did not want something in return.* He has learned to give hugs, to give a friendly kiss on the cheek, to give "high fives", but they appear to be rote, and void of any real emotional attachment and only occur when the situation suggests it is to his advantage.

Does Shane experience emotion? I can definitely say "yes!" I've watched his face, his demeanor during and after an event. He feels very deeply. He is unable to express. When sad or disappointed, he will put his head down, take a deep breath, then close his eyes and lean his head back as he 'stabilizes'. Except for the physical aggression and self-injurious behaviors, I would say his coping mechanism is excellent. It is during times of sadness, disappointment, aloneness, that I want to reach out to him, offering comfort. But he cannot allow me into his realm.

Last year he came to the sofa where I was sitting and quietly sat down, very close. He took my hand and looked at me intently. After a few moments, he clearly spoke, "I want to die." I talked to him about death and it just not being 'his time' yet. It is difficult for a parent to realize the depths of a child's anguish.

In minutes, he was up and laughing again. The episode prompted a trip to his psychiatrist and, when asked if he was ever sad, he repeated, "sad". An anti-depressant was prescribed and perhaps it's helped. I don't know. Since that time, we've decreased the dosage due to the weight gain. Most of his medications have an adverse effect on his weight. And of course the weight gain causes additional health difficulties. It's the ever popular Catch-22.

He continues to observe the world around him intently while appearing to ignore his surroundings. He is constantly listening to conversations taking place. It may appear he's sitting quietly playing with his security shoestring, but nothing escapes his vigilant mind. He absorbs the activities of his surrounding environment as surely as a sponge takes in moisture. I observed him actually looking AT and watching a news telecast one day. I wonder how much he actually understands with regards to current events in the world. He does not verbalize and I will never know.

Although it is apparent to those of us who know him well that he understands all conversation around him, he reacts with indifference. Sometimes I will notice 'that certain look' on his face and tell him, "You are thinking. I can see the wheels turning." He smiles. We both understand. Yes, the thought process is alive and well.

I am constantly amazed at positioned and experienced people who continue to talk in abstract sentences to autistic persons. I am angered and confused by the people who speak '*about*' my son while in his presence, instead of speaking *to* him. He hates meetings. For three decades, he has been the subject of more meetings than I (or he) would care to recall. I know how I were to feel if people gathered around the table to discuss my behaviors, bowel habits, food preferences, to name a few of the activities which make us, 'us'. He can't contribute to the conversation. He cannot verbally defend or validate what is being said about him. It is no wonder he hates the process. Now when we have quarterly meetings for him, he usually stays only long enough to observe who is in attendance. Then he adamantly demands a car ride.

He has no interests in life, save for going for car rides or enjoying the sensory activity of playing in a mound of stuffed animals. He does also enjoy going shopping and looking for things he might purchase. Therefore, it has become the mission of family and staff to offer *what we can,* attempting to keep him interested in life and smiling. We do have those days when I would equate the situation as his being a prince, being at his beck and call to fan him with peacock feather fans and feed him peeled grapes (and cheese).

Shane still demands 100% of his caregiver's attention. If he feels attention is being given to something else, he may intentionally go into another area of the house to deliberately soil or to tear one of his possessions. Sometimes just cooking a meal for him requires the fine art of juggling attentions. His deliberate acts of soiling or destruction may be due to his wanting to 'car ride' during a busy time, or it may be simply an outward expression of his ornery streak. Either way, he appears to enjoy the negative reaction from his caregivers.

While he cannot function well in crowded situations, it sometimes appears he wants to keep those closest to him 'all to and for himself'. He is adamant that people cannot talk too long on the phone, or in any other manner divert their attentions to anything else but him. I don't know where autism ends and 'just being demanding' starts. I don't know if there is a difference between the two. Perhaps he has a deep rooted fear of losing the attentions of those people who establish a link between 'his world' and 'ours'. Perhaps he feels that if he allows people to have interests other than him, he will be left behind. I don't have answers and probably never will.

His baseball caps and selected shoestrings have been and will probably remain his islands of comfort and security throughout life.

It also appears Shane 'tunes into' the energies and moods of those persons around him. Even though he is at the mercy of so many factors that affect his demeanor, we attempt to be passive. It is advantageous to present an 'in control' and calm demeanor that he can 'draw' upon. It doesn't always work, but is worth the effort. It may alleviate his self-abuse and aggression, but it can also wear very thin on one's own psyche. Suppression and denial of emotions and feelings are a major factor in stress. While this technique is good for Shane, it is hard on those of us accommodating his needs.

Television does not hold his interests, save for a few commercials and an occasional basketball game or soccer game. Many years ago, watching 'Name That Tune' would peak his interest for the duration of the show. He loved it! We taped a few episodes so he could continue to watch them repeatedly. Then a direct care attendant taped over his prized possessions. The attendant had used them selfishly to tape late night wrestling matches. I can forgive a lot of people for an array of issues, but I still struggle with that one.

He also likes 'The Price Is Right'. However, he tends to become too 'hyped' and may go into that 'out of control' mode. We have to monitor his viewing and may turn the show off until he is able to self-calm. We've taped several episodes. This time his long-time staff broke the tabs off of the tapes so no one could tape over his episodes. I doubt that Bob Barker ever had a more avid fan. He watched with extreme concentration when Drew

Carey took over the program, then smiled and accepted the change.

Shane cannot tolerate activities that involve over stimulation, either in the number of persons present at an event or activity, or activities he is simply not interested in. He appears to see no value in attending events such as picnics, carnivals, neighborhood 'walks', family gatherings, or other community functions that may be available to him. If Shane cannot attend functions, then neither can the rest of us when he is in our care. Hence, the family also experiences isolation. There is always time when direct care staff are caring for his needs, but I am usually too exhausted from the day's duties to attend even the most relaxing event. Mike and I usually go for an afternoon walk, but I am inclined to become indolent in the evenings.

Unless (and IF!) a visitor would come to see Shane exclusively and unless it is someone he considers to be *his* personal friend, he is not particularly interested in that person's presence in his home. It is his apartment, his home. If old friends think I am evasive when they offer to 'stop by for coffee or tea and chat' when I am with Shane, it is only because I respect his right to decline visitors. He does not like to share the attentions of his care givers with other people.

Shane occasionally requests beer. I have would have no qualms about allowing my thirty-two year old son to drink; he is certainly old enough. However, there is the medication regime to consider as alcohol enhances the effects of many of his current medications. Shane is encouraged to make as many choices as can be presented in every area of his life; that is the respected rule. There are also exceptions to every rule. Many years ago Miles and I became Shane's co-guardians. We intervene. Even though Shane's physicians have given 'permission' to allow Shane an *occasional* beer, we only allow 'near-beer'. When I say occasional, I would say he actually has one near-beer in every four to six weeks. Even with this slight alteration, having his requested beverage on special occasions seems to be alright with him. Shane is aware of the difference between regular beer and the altered near-beer, but is usually satisfied with the compromise.

Shane is an avid collector of balls. They include baseballs, basketballs, soccer balls and play balls. If he has spending money, he will choose little balls, large balls, plain ones and decorated ones. On a visit to Grandma at the first nursing home she was in, he snatched an exercise ball from the hands of one of the elderly ladies there. He clung to it and screamed refusing to relinquish it to the lady, the aides, or to me. We finally agreed he could take it home. Later I returned it to the lady he'd taken it from.   The universe and all that lays within is HIS oyster.

He used to watch sporting events on television with one of his staff. It appeared he actually enjoyed basketball, football and soccer. I think it was because of the balls involved. The only time a behavioral specialist took him to a basketball game, he practically tore the poor man to shreds. While Shane was excited to go, he could not tolerate the crowds and noise. They had to leave after only a few minutes. The man who accompanied him came home with scratches, bite marks, and a new understanding of what Shane could and could not tolerate.

On a good day he requests constant car rides. Even his favorite activity has its limitations.   So we drive the same streets and highways continually. Fortunately we don't have to drive the same routes and can add a degree of 'difference' to our outings as long as it is within a safe radius of home. He's an excellent navigator and knows 'what's where' very well. When in any given neighborhood, he will start naming the grocery stores or drug stores that are in the area, knowing where they are and how to get to them.

One might rationalize that his love of car rides would lend to our having the luxury of taking road trips which we all might enjoy. This is not so, for an array of reasons. He cannot tolerate driving more than twenty or so miles from home. To 'vacation' and spend time away from home is absolutely out of his scope of safety and tolerance. There are the mood swings which may leave us frantically searching for the fastest route home; minutes can make a great difference! Secondly, not all stores have 'family friendly' bathroom facilities. There's also the simple and plain fact that if he knows it somewhere *you* would like to go, something *you* would like to see, then it is his duty to rebel and refuse.

If he needs to return home or doesn't feel well, he may say, "home", or just unbuckle his seatbelt. He might also strike out at the driver. Having a childproof lock on the door closest him is a requirement I demand of anyone who may transport him. He has been known to open the door, or at least attempt to, while the car is in motion. I have noticed he may (or may not) check his seatbelt before he tries to open the door. It appears the act is to upset the driver. It's that negative attention thing.

I would like to take him to a live concert. Perhaps his love for the performance would override his inability to handle crowds once again. But as his motor skills have decreased, so has his stamina. He tires more easily. He is content with his car rides and occasional shopping trips. Perhaps if I offered the use of our garage to a young rock band Shane would enjoy a performance sans the external hassle. Our neighbors are very nice people, but I'm not sure they'd appreciate our efforts (smile). Actually, we have a few neighbors who might actually enjoy the gesture.

Shane breaks life down to basics. He presents with an honest intent in all that he does, whether it is a positive or a negative situation. He is not encumbered with the 'niceties' of society, nor the ritualistic acts of etiquette our world adheres to. An example that comes to mind is that he knows to shake hands when meeting a person. If he has taken a dislike to the new person, he will not shake hands. There is a basic honesty to his interactions with people and also in his approach to life in general. He excels in the areas of what he understands and accepts, ignoring the areas in which he has no control or vested interest. He has learned to balk at areas that cause him stress. While many people present our own varied facades to the world, he does not. Perhaps we could all learn from his basic, honest approach to life.

At the time of this writing, he can still ambulate around the house with help from handrails in the hallway. However, there are also days when he requires the support of staff to avoid falling. The quality of his ambulation within his home also falls victim to 'when all systems are…go'.

His abilities are extensive. He can help to cook, clean, to perform many self-help skills *when he chooses*. However, when the outside and internal factors are affecting him, he is unable to complete the simplest task without escalating behaviors, which can be lead to his being out of control. We have learned when to elicit his participation, and when to allow him space so he can self compose and calm the inner battles which he fights on a daily basis.

Summer is usually the kindest season for and to Shane. Spring allergies accompanied by the earth molds are his worst enemy. During the rest of the year, we are at the mercy of other allergies, seasonal affect disorder, erratic depakote levels, sinus difficulties, barometric pressures, and his inability to communicate which of the afore mentioned conditions are effecting him.

Vacillating between 'somewhat normal' demeanors and periods of fears, there are also episodes of the 'manic' stage. It is during these times of uncontrollable laughter and screaming that breakage of targeted household items takes place. We keep all coffee cups secure in the dishwasher, dirty or clean. He is selective in breaking items and will find great glee in destroying something he knows is of value to you, whether it is sentimental value, or just an item one might use a lot. This is another reason I could not, would not, live with Shane. Instinctively, he would destroy every material possession I could have. He seems to like his apartment. It is tastefully decorated (my opinion) in neutral color tones. Most of the decorations are non-breakable. When he shows interest in destroying any particular item, it is simply removed from his environment.

When he is in a manic, destructive mode, he will tear his own favorite shirts or personal items while laughing hysterically. Material possessions are of little value to him, save for his treasured shoestrings and hats, which give him comfort and security while navigating through life. All staff are to carry, in their car, an emergency sheet which gives basic information on Shane, should there be an accident. On this sheet his picture appears with address, contact information, diagnosis, medications required, and, at the bottom, the notation that under no circumstance should his hat be taken away from him.

Certain phrases need to be repeated back to him. These include "Oh ho ho, Mommy's little Frenchman.", "Ho ho ho, green giant.", and "You have a nice day!", among others. I look at these phrases as some sort of mental road sign, or concrete mental marker. It appears that repeating these phrases back to him allows him the reassurance that he is making connection with the person he is with. Perhaps it helps him to connect with our reality.

We also go through a wide range of "How many…(pan pizzas, strawberry ice cream, green beans, mashed potatoes, etc., etc., and ETC.!). When I am pumping gas for the car, Shane will sit inside and start the "how many" regime. People in the area cannot hear him, but do hear me echoing his verbalization. So I stand there loudly spewing phrases like "How many avocado?" and "How many coconut cake?" to what other customers would perceive to be thin air.

It has only been recently that he started to let us know the answer is "five". There are always five green bean, five mash potato, five pan pizzas, five strawberry shortcakes. I wouldn't attempt to change his answer. That would confuse him. It is all right if there are always five chicken soup, five coconut cake and five of any edible substance he can mention.

Yesterday he intentionally and gleefully poured Mike's reserved glass of water onto the car floor. He stated, "I spilled the water." It doesn't matter that he actually spilled the water. The car floor is quite used to mishaps of all kinds. I was merely pleased to hear his proper use of the pronoun, "I". It is times like that which offer some insight into his 'lost' language. He's there, inside somewhere, struggling to be heard.

Had I known autistic individuals generally learn a word, and then retain that word for the rest of their lives, I may have handled our conversations differently. At some point along Shane's journey, a staff taught him to say "poop" for feces. I find the word extremely distasteful and cringe every time we're in public when Shane calls out (usually loudly), "Go poop!". I would encourage young mothers to use proper English when teaching their autistic child toileting words or it may come back to haunt them in future years.

Between the younger years and adolescence, Shane began echoing the last few words of what had been said to him.

The only singular words which came easily to him were names of certain foods and the fast food restaurants he liked. But he retained the ability to name objects when looking at a picture, which he could do as a toddler. To determine what Shane wanted, you would ask (i.e.), "Do you want macaroni?" If the answer was yes, he would repeat, "macaroni." If the answer was no, he would remain silent.

When he was approximately twenty-five years of age, he was having supper with staff when one asked him if he wanted fried chicken. Shane yelled, "NO!". Since that time, he has retained the ability to let us know when the answer is no. When the answer is 'yes', he still repeats the last words of our question. On a good day when 'all systems are go', he may independently venture with, "I want fish (or whatever)."

He is, as are most persons struggling with autism, very literal. In attempts to be conversational with Shane, an occasional person might ask him (i.e. "Do you like ice cream?"). At that point, he expects them to give him ice cream. He hears 'like' and he hears 'ice cream'. He understands it is a question. He does not appear to understand why someone would ask him a question and then pull the subject away from him.

Just last week I heard someone ask if he liked to shop at (Store X). He took their hand. He was ready for them to take him to Store X. The lady had asked if he liked Store X and Shane perceived it to be an *invitation to actually go* to store X. She thought his response was 'cute'. He was confused and frustrated. The lady has worked with an array of disabilities, inclusive of autism, for many years. He needs to hear concrete vocalizations. He does not understand abstract terms. I am an abstract thinker, but have learned to flip-flop to concrete verbalization when talking to my son.

As a general rule, he is good-natured and very patient with us. It took months before we realized "apple-be-day" meant he wanted us to bake a cake (Happy Birthday). His requests for "t-giraffe" were a great mystery for many years before he pointed to a Toys-R-Us store and loudly yelled, "t-giraffe". Sometimes we're just slow in figuring things out.

When 'all systems are go', he is able to communicate his wants/needs by saying clue words, such as "key" or "car ride" when he wants to ride. During the times those phrases aren't available to him, he may substitute a word, such as "coat". Family and staff understand "coat" means "get your coat and we can go for a car ride". It doesn't matter if it's mid-summer and he does not need the coat…it still means he wants to go for a ride.

He may look for a jacket to wear in mid-summer, or attempt to go outside in a T-shirt during the coldest winter months.

I say the phrases aren't always available to him because what he is actually thinking may not come to him to vocalize properly. We've heard about a dozen complete, complex structured sentences in his life. We KNOW his mind is capable, but something short circuits in the process.

Various speech pathologists in Shane's life have chastised me for having taught him a very limited amount 'total communication', which combined the use of sign language and verbalization. Several therapists had told me since Shane had the ability to speak, we should not allow him to rely on signing words. I am very sorry I listened to their advice. So much of his frustration comes from the inability to produce the correct word for any given item or occasion. Even now he occasionally amuses himself by signing the different colors and saying the word, which he expects us to repeat. If we sign the word for any particular color, he is able to immediately recall the word. We've tried to reintroduce signing into his life, but he isn't interested. Another window closed.

If we are experiencing a day when we *have* to go to the post office, or bank and he is not in the mood to go, we may as well forget it or wait until back up staff can be present. Due to his erratic sleep pattern and mood swings, many duties are put on hold. It's all a matter of keeping the priorities straight.

He is unable to attend workshops for the handicapped and similar activities without creating safety issues, both to himself and to other participants. Frustration is created, even by having too many people in his home for his own required meetings. He picks and chooses whom he will allow into his world. He adamantly protects his world against anyone and anything that may interfere with his ability to assimilate. Life with Shane is isolation. It probably isn't half of the isolation he feels. His presence draws you into his world.

He has little to no control over external factors. Therefore, he has always struggled to have control by controlling those around him. In the institution, as well as under agency rules, the masses had to follow the programming. That is, there were time constraints on activities, eating, sleeping. Shane could not adapt. The square pegs being forced into round holes met with a lot of resistance. By allowing Shane to sleep, eat, and go for car rides when he chooses, he no longer needs to fight the system. That doesn't mean there aren't rules. For example, a staff may say, "O.K., 2 car rides tonight." Period. He can tolerate the wait if he knows there's something in the deal for him.

Staff vary in their expectations of Shane, as well as the limitations they impose. Shane knows where each person draws the line. He accepts what each staff offers as long as he knows what to expect in advance. One staff may allow for numerous car rides during his shift while another staff may limit the rides at two. Knowing exactly what his staff will allow offers him some control over his daily schedule, as erratic as it may be.

Unfortunately the external factors as well as internal demons continue to plague him. Since 2004, his neurological functioning, particularly the gross motor movements, have continually declined. These subtle 'spirals' of loss do occur, independent of our vigilant watches over his depakote levels and continual monitoring by his neurologist. Each spiral downward is preceded by slight tremors of his extremities. It is usually of his left arm and hand. They usually occur during his sleep and are followed by a slight, but noticeable loss of functioning of that side. After a few days of an increase in loss of gait and balance, he appears to 'plateau', regaining some agility, but never returning to the point of what it was before the tremors began.

Shane is very aware his body is failing him. He is angry and frustrated by the loss of gross motor skills. With his fears and frustration, we notice an increase in his aggression and self-injurious behaviors. Somehow, he manages to adapt to the changes. As he matures, he adamantly attempts to present a pleasant demeanor when he can.   Beneath the autism, my son is an extremely good-natured human being. He always seems to accept, after a period of time, the ongoing decrease of his body strength and agility. But he tires easily now and requires additional sleep.

Had it not been for the internal turmoil of 'autism', I believe he would have been an average but handsome, intelligent and humorous young man. His interests might have remained as they stand today, in the realm of sports, cars, ladies…and beer. But that is in the realm of what might have been. We live with the reality of his limitations.

For the most part, he meets life with a smile, which is probably more than I would do if I were to walk in his proverbial shoes. Upon awakening, at whatever hour of the day or night, he faces a world that he doesn't fit into. It surely must be overwhelming. Fear and frustration drive his life, in a degree that is unfamiliar to most of us. He, and those who share his destiny, are some of the most courageous and bravest souls one may ever have the pleasure of meeting.

He also continues to be a perplexing and complicated young man. Recently his staff came in while Shane was asleep in his bedroom. The direct care had brought a chocolate bar they thought they could eat if Shane slept during their 'shift'. Respecting my requests that Shane should not eat chocolate products, they hid their candy on the top shelf of the kitchen cupboard behind some boxes of tea without saying a word. When Shane awoke and came into the kitchen, he went directly to the cupboard, moved the boxes of tea and requested "Cholat". He could have found the chocolate by acute sense of smell. I would rather think it was because of 'acute perception'.

Since most of his observable senses appear to be 'heightened', it would not be unusual to rationalize that his access to other 'senses' are also highly developed. I do not profess to know how my son perceives the world around him. When I attempt to understand by asking him, he only looks at me and smiles. Sometimes he laughs at me. Perhaps the only answer is, "It's 53, Stupid!"

Shane has made tremendous progress since we started the home program under Indiana's Waiver Program. The primary factor which has been the driving force in Shane's progress is that he has more control over what he needs in his life's journey. He does not have to adhere to routines that are necessary to meet the needs of anyone but himself

A secondary factor in his ongoing progress is that we have been able to monitor Shane's health needs in a constant and timely manner. If he lets us know he has a headache, we are able to address the need upon command. If he indicates his ears hurt, it is addressed immediately. We are on a first name basis with the physician's nurses and can readily schedule an appointment if necessary.

The third factor I would consider most critical to his success is that we have created an environment of safety. He is assured there will be no further physical, emotional, verbal or sexual abuse. By having *consistent, understanding direct care staff*, I am confident he feels safe and secure in his home. He knows what to expect from each person and no longer has to be fearful of 'just anyone' coming in to cover a particular shift to work with him.

Part III

Three decades of observation
and the ramblings of a senior citizen

For any family (or agency) that may have doubts about the safety of their people, I would urge the purchase and use of a security system. The cameras are relatively inexpensive and can alleviate any doubts regarding the care being given. With the current staff working with Shane, I don't always have the cameras in operation. Rather, they are turned on at random to monitor if he should fall or injure himself as his mobility declines. The cameras are always in place and can be utilized should I feel they need be, or if Shane gives any indication of being uncomfortable with his environment. I do not have a camera in his bedroom because I respect his adult male need for privacy.

Shane is actually being served with less funding than when he was a resident of the institutions. We do not have the need to maintain large housing facility with separate buildings to provide the various programming needs. We do not have grounds keepers nor do we have a maintenance department to support. I am the person who oversees those responsibilities. We do not have a housekeeping department. His staff and I are responsible for the cleanliness of his home. We do not have an array of administrative assistants in our home to coordinate our internal paperwork. I assume responsibility for overseeing and collecting the required data. There is no need for a payroll department; it is my responsibility to write the checks to the direct care contractors. I am also the personnel department in charge of monitoring, hiring and firing direct care contractors.

I have assumed the role of health care coordinator for his physician, medical specialist and dental appointments. Medication orders, deliveries and documentation requires constant attention. I believe we have been able to monitor his health issues better than some of the programs previously presented. We do not require an array of supervisors to oversee his programming. As co-guardians, Miles and I assume that role.

We have always had the good fortune of having excellent case managers who oversee his waiver status. His current case manager is a grand lady and friend who is deeply involved with the disabled population, both professionally and personally. She works with us to implement creative and cost effective programming. The programming is tailored to be exclusively for Shane, his needs and his choices.

I am rarely asked now what I 'do', or what I 'did' for a living. I've reached the status of being a senior citizen and it is assumed I am retired. If I am asked, I am at loss for an answer. I suppose I am a stay-at-home mom.

Even at my age, I sometimes look at our present world in disbelief and confusion. I continue to be disappointed and disillusioned by the fact that everything in our lives seems to be dependent on money. I wonder where our priorities lie. It would appear that as a society, we have not progressed in eradicating greed and the need to be 'superior'. We are still the herd at the watering hole fighting and kicking to dominate the resources.

Our handicapped population, our elderly, and our most vulnerable are on the bottom rung of our society's priorities. I believe the Federal and State governments are allocating funding to the people in the most efficient manner currently possible. It comes down to a matter of economics. Those of the population who cannot financially contribute to the wealth of the nation are left to receive the crumbs of the financially empowered. Those who take from the money pot as opposed to giving (i.e. the handicapped, the homeless, or the elderly) are simply not good business in the eyes of (some of) the politicians who make legislative decisions on our peoples' behalf.

People who go into the social work field usually do so because they sincerely want to help those of the population who are less fortunate. They see a need and want to create change. They are acutely aware they won't be among the wealthy elite. Due to the demands of the population, many start with high aspirations and energy. They are the teachers, the case managers, the direct care aides and others from an array of social service professions. A great number of these good people 'burn out' rapidly. It is a challenging and incredibly demanding field.

Historically, we have made some fairly dramatic changes in the attitudes about and the care of the vulnerable. When the hunter-gathers existed, those who could no longer contribute to the well-being of the tribe were left behind. Later societies would simply kill a child born with mental deficits, or they would be taken away somewhere and left to die. Then came the early institutions, complete with leg irons and cages. It has only been relatively recent that society came to realize these very unfortunate souls were worthy of more than just contempt and loathing. Still, a number of the handicapped population continue to live in forgotten isolation, away from the eyes of society.

I also remain concerned as to how we can channel the progressive and positive attitude of those in administrative positions to the front-line people, the direct care staff. The pay involved for direct care workers is low. It is considered to be a non-skilled field. As a society, we place more financial value on someone who builds technical machinery than on the person who is responsible for the health and safety of another human being.

The low pay rate has created its own monster. While there are good and caring people who continue to work in the field, they struggle to make the financial ends meet. Yet because it is classified as a 'non-skilled' area of employment, it has also been a beacon for an army of people who have no interest in being of service to our handicapped population. These people flood the workforce because of the increasing demand for direct care personnel.

I have been told that low performance (of some) direct care staff can be salvaged with retraining. Yet I find that most of the negative aspects of direct care givers lays in the area of their *attitude*. How do you change or retrain the *attitude* of people? How do we draw qualified, caring people? I don't have answers. If a higher pay rate is presented, we may very well end up with a lot of overpaid people who continue to have a detrimental attitude and substandard performance. By the same standard, the low pay rate is unfair to those qualified caregivers whose services and attitudes are beyond reproach.

Of all the services given to our fragile population, the one of most concern is the direct care staff. They are on the front lines. They are the people who determine if the needs of the clients are truly being met. They are the people who ultimately determine if clients have positive or negative experiences in their lives. Unless, and until, this field can offer an abundance of qualified and caring staff, then we as a society and as a system have failed our people. If the high expectations and aspirations of the administrative force do not filter down to the direct care attendants, we have nothing.

There are many people working in the field of direct care. There are the 'good guys' who give of themselves and truly make a positive difference in the lives of the people they serve. As I have stated before, these people are overworked and underpaid. They are the angels of the field. They are in a category unto themselves.

The second category of direct care staff includes the 'warm bodies'. It appears they only work in the field of service because they 1.) cannot find employment elsewhere or 2.) believe it's easily attainable employment where they can perform minimal work while they talk the game of competence to their supervisors.

The third category frightens me. They are the mean spirited people. It appears they work in the field because they feel superior to those they serve. It also appears they enjoy dominance over a population that cannot stand up to them.

It would be grand if the 'good apples' could weed out the 'bad apples'. Unfortunately, I have noted all too often examples of a group of incompetent staff banding together to expel a good person from a home. The competent staff is usually pushed out of the care giving group because they refuse to join the band of 'slackers'. Supervisors are all too often verbally courted by the group. This leaves the competent staff with little to no support. Many good staff have been fired or forced to leave due to circumstances far beyond their control.

I would say, however, that several staff are no longer with us after observation of the security tapes or actual viewing staff performance. In 2004 I observed a staff asleep in the recliner as Shane slept on the sofa. The staff and I came to an immediate agreement that he should resign as he was working too many hours with another client. He could not give Shane the attention we required. Six hours later, Shane had one of the two grand mal seizures we experienced. Had I not been watching and had the seizure occurred when staff dozed, the outcome could have been disastrous.

Another staff left our household after I viewed their use of our computer, printer and at least a ream of printer paper being consumed for projects he was engaged in for his personal use. That would be the same staff who would hide Shane's shoes when he didn't want to take him for a ride. Shane would search the house frantically for hours to look for socks and shoes. Talk about frustration! That little tidbit surfaced upon review of tapes I had recorded, via the security system.

While under the care of an agency (I certainly wouldn't have hired this one!), we had another interesting experience with a staff. The lady was quite verbal in telling everyone she was sent by God to save Shane from the other staff and from his programming errors. She hovered over him so intensely and constantly that he could not move freely around his home. She washed his hands and mouth after every bite of food. She talked and rambled on to him continually about how she was his savior. Within two weeks, she was literally cowering on the floor, asking Shane why he didn't like her when she'd done everything for him. He had to be pulled away to save her from being hit repeatedly.

Another lady lost her place at our house when she walked off of her shift at 2:00 in the morning. She called me to come in to cover the remainder of her hours, but already had her coat on, backing out the door while making feeble excuses when I arrived. Shane was awake at the time, watching and listening as she told us it was all Shane's fault. She just couldn't 'take it anymore'. He liked the woman and his behaviors with her had been, for the most part, very good. The hurt, confused and betrayed look on Shane's face spoke volumes as she blamed him for her leaving. I was aware she had a lot of 'personal baggage', but her main reason for leaving at that very moment was that her involvement with a new love interest was more pressing than holding down a position. It wasn't until later that we discovered how many groceries were missing from our home. She was good, in a sneaky sense, in her pillage of the pantry. We never did spot the groceries actually walking out the door under the eye of the cameras.

We've had some very interesting applicants. One lady came into Shane's home and immediately told him he'd have to lose the hat, that it was totally inappropriate to wear a hat indoors. Talk about stepping on the hooves of a sacred cow! She then proceeded to sit in Shane's recliner, even though I told her that was where he preferred to sit. With an armload of credentials, references, and past experience, she informed us that she would soon have him going to any community programming she chose and that he WOULD conform. By mid visit, he had firmly but gently taken a hold of her arm and was repeating, "Go!, Go!" She didn't call back, which spared me from any further contact with her.

When choosing direct care personnel for your person, one must be vigilant and informed. Family members are usually good candidates, as they know where your person has been and what the expectations are. In my opinion, experience doesn't always mean diddly. Sometimes 'experienced' and 'book-learned' people come with preconceived notions about what they should or will accomplish. Some of the best people we've had came with absolutely no experience in the field. They were good people who could adhere to State regulations, and understood the methods that have proven to be successful for Shane. They were eager to provide the services required of them and seemed to be genuinely interested in the welfare of the people they were helping.

We've had good experience with people who treat Shane as a 'regular Joe', rather than treating him as a handicapped person.

If a person comes to me with an armload of credentials and experience, I am wary. I cringe when they start telling me how great they are. When they are more concerned with tooting their own horn instead of listening to Shane's needs, I do not consider them.

Condescending people can also be detrimental to your programming. For as long as my son can independently dress himself, fix his own toast (again, when all systems are 'go'), and perform tasks, then I feel it's good for his self esteem to do so. The day may come when he is no longer able to perform such tasks, but his abilities must be respected until, unless, the day comes when he is no longer to do so. He responds well to people who treat him as 'just another guy', but will support him in the areas where he knows he requires support. He is a 32 year-old man, trapped within his self. He is of high intellect, understanding all adult conversation and should not be 'spoken down to', nor be addressed in a manner of how one might speak to a toddler. While his expressive language may be appear child-like, he is not. Shane must be allowed to do all he is capable of doing. His quality of life and perhaps even his survival within another system may depend on it.

Our best regulator when choosing a new staff is to let Shane make the final cut. The approval of a person, or disapproval, may be subtle, but it is there. Gushy people who come in claiming to be his best buddy on the first visit leave him cold. They leave me chilled, also! The introduction of new staff into his life is a slow process, although Shane has a gift for judging the true nature of any person. He may quietly watch a person for a few minutes before making a conscious decision to accept, or veto them. I value his choices and, in retrospect, admit he has made wise choices when I have been deceived by the first appearances of people. Being highly intuitive, he has made the decision of 'yea' or 'nay' long before they formed their opinion of him. He is picky. Considering the past experiences he has endured, he has a right to choose. He *knows*.

As a parent, you are not going to find direct care staff who will agree with you unconditionally or who would interact with your child exactly as you do. For that, you'll have to clone. Shane's health and safety needs are first and foremost, and as long as direct care staff adheres to State guidelines and also have met Shane's criteria, I am an 'o.k.' camper. If they stick around long enough to actually get to know and bond with Shane, then I am a 'happy' camper. I talked with one mother who wanted staff to not only meet all of the required criteria, but to also iron her son's shirts daily. She's probably still looking for help.

Shane is extremely fortunate to have the direct care staff currently working with him. They are all very different in their personalities and interests. Each person in brings a positive aspect of their individual personality to share with him. Everyone currently in Shane's life has been through the spectrum of his health issues, behaviors and demeanors. He is comfortable in knowing he won't face retaliation for any aggression which might occur during his off-the-wall phases. I believe it is because of his natural good nature, his amiability, sense of humor, and general personality that entice his direct care staff to remain with him.

I am grateful to L.G. and Stan, who have worked with Shane on a long-time basis. I can only hope they realize how very valuable and appreciated they are. We always seem to have need for a third contractor. The people who have filled this position have been good people; Shane has benefited from their presence and has enjoyed his time with them. However, that position seems to be in the revolving-door mode and either Miles or I sporadically need to cover the vacancy.

The rule is that Shane and his needs are the prime responsibilities. Keeping his environment clean is also something that should be accomplished when (and if) he sleeps. The contract drawn at time of accepting an independent contractor's terms is inclusive of keeping Shane's environment clean and sanitary. I have a 'list' available of light housekeeping chores which need to be routinely performed. I've completed the entire list myself in thirty minutes or less. I don't care how they accomplish the tasks as long as the household environment is clean and sanitary. It isn't important that swabbing the toilet bowl isn't done with complete perfection, just as long as someone at least tried. Clean is a subjective term. What looks clean to one person may not be acceptable to another. Sometimes you just have to roll with the tide and compromise.

When Shane is asleep, I am o.k. with staff watching television, reading, or chatting on their cell phones. It is acceptable as long as they regularly monitor his respiration periodically and make sure he is resting comfortably. It is those times when Shane has slept for five hours and the staff has watched television for five hours that I get a little testy. I also become disagreeable if there are signs of Shane being left to fend for himself because staff are busy watching television.

The major difficulty I note with home services is the availability of staff. It is particularly difficult for those of us who do not have extended family to draw from. I interview, screen, collect needed requirements, accept an independent contractor's terms and sometimes dismiss. The hardest part is just finding independent consultants who actually fulfill the necessary requirements. The job market isn't exactly saturated with people who really want to work with autism.

It is at this point that I must say home programming is not for everyone. I have met many people who were not only comfortable and secure, but also very happy with life in a group home. If Shane were open to that possibility, it would be my programming of choice. However, he has shown us that he cannot tolerate that particular situation. He thrives on the home programming and family involvement and I will attempt to work with him as long as I can.

When determining what your person needs, the dynamics of the **entire** family must be taken into consideration. If any family members in the home are placed into serious jeopardy or are living in fear of their sibling or afflicted family member, there is no recourse other than placement out of the home. When Shane was younger, home programming was simply not available. If it had been, I do not feel I could have considered it. We did not have the option of keeping Shane in our home setting. His violence had thrown our small family into the danger zone. We lacked the safety nets, financial resources, and we were depleted of energy.

By virtue of Shane's mellowing, of becoming older, we are able to accomplish what we are currently doing. Had I kept him with us in the younger, uncontrollable times, it would have been a great compromise to the health and safety of us all. Every option must be weighed. The safety and well being of <u>all</u> family members <u>must</u> be taken into consideration.

Once you get over the guilt feelings of 'having put your child away' and take a look in retrospect, you will realize there is no right, no wrong in the decision you may make. *No right, no wrong.* Some decisions in life are just like that.

So many things have changed since we started on our journey. Programming is now available for persons with autism. Not only have early intervention programs increased in number, but also programs that offer respite care for parents. Public schools have added autism to their special education vocabulary.

When Shane was young, we would be asked, "What's wrong with your child?" People can be so insensitive and just damned blunt. I'd tell them he was autistic. I was usually told something like, "Oh, well my grandson likes to draw, too!". That's autistic, not artistic, you idiot! Or that's what I would like to have said to them. I usually said nothing. In 'the old days', no one would understand. Times have certainly changed.

I have stated that my son has autism. I have also stated he is autistic. The latter statement is in these current times, politically incorrect. There are some people who take offense at their person being called autistic because it is supposed to be 'person first, disability second'.

I am very fortunate in *not* having diabetes. However if I did, I would have no difficulty in telling someone, 'I am a diabetic' or 'I am a person with diabetes'. We began our years before political correctness was an issue. My son has always been person first, regardless of our situation or his placement. That is how it should be for all people, whether they have any type of handicap or not. It is the respect we give rather than the word usage we choose.

With regards to my son's condition, words and diagnoses are simply words. I have neither the interest nor energy to mince. My sentiment is that a rose by any other name……

I am very pleased to observe that administration in our State system and public school systems are emphasizing the personal needs of the individual rather than 'group' programming. It appears noted changes are being organized in many agencies. I can only hope this positive move is taking place. Programming has taken on overtures of taking on a creative and innovative approach to serving our population. There is a certain 'understanding' of the needs of our children that was not available just two decades ago. Slowly, with the perseverance of kindly souls in the social field, we continue to make positive changes for the care of our vulnerable populations. We still have a very long way to go.

For the first five or six years of Shane's life, I lived in denial. Determination to find a cure, a therapy, a medication, anything, filled my life. Somewhere during those years, guilt also surfaced. What had I done to jeopardize my son? The guilt dissipates over time. I have met many parents of children with autism. We come from all backgrounds, races, religions and beliefs. I have never met anyone who intentionally or knowingly caused their offspring to be autistic.

Then there were many years filled with anger. How could any god be so cruel as to allow this malady to take my son from me? It wasn't until he was in his late teens that I accepted things 'just are'. I think it's alright to live the grieving process, to feel it, but there is also a time to move on. Acceptance is a good stage. Later, and I'm not sure when, I began to feel a tremendous pride in my son.

I don't think, if I had life to live over, that I would make any major changes. I have never met anyone that I would even consider changing places with. The minor changes I would make would be few, but perhaps significant. I would have insisted Shane be placed on seizure medication at an early age, because I believe, whatever the etiology, *something* is causing frontal lobe seizures. I would have used holistic methods in accompaniment of allopathic medications more often to ease his discomfort. I would have been adamant in our efforts to teach him total communication. There is nothing like hindsight!

Coping is quite another story. When I had Shane at home when he was younger, there was no time for meditation or even relaxation techniques. Even now the time away comes in the form of stolen moments. It was, and sometimes still is, simply a matter of putting one foot in front of the other. At various times of my life, I have considered taking a prescription anti-depressant or anti-anxiety medication. But that isn't an option for me. While growing up, I watched a family member become addicted to over-the-counter medications. She wasn't ill, but took the medications so she wouldn't *become* ill. The experience left me with distaste for taking any medications at all. However, I do know many, many mothers who would swear that anti-depressant prescriptions hold them together. I have a profound respect for people who do seek medical advice, whether it be homeopathic or allopathic, in times of stress.

It is….interesting and perhaps distressing to note that we evidently have become a medicated society. Television, our mass media leader, now advises us via commercials on how to 'cope' with everything from depression to impotency. Being older allows me to remember when television was for the purpose of entertainment and news, with informative commercials letting us know of the newest food or toothpaste products. It is apparent we now need all of the help we can get to cope, to just get through the day. It would appear pills are the solution to any and all ordinary, everyday crises. In our efforts to escape our 'realities', I wonder what happened to just facing and dealing with situations. On a day-to-day basis, do we really need to be numbed and subdued to face life's challenges? I would think medication should be the exception for required situations, not the rule of thumb for everyone. Of course I am speaking only of the rather ordinary circumstances. Extreme situations do indeed call for extraordinary measures.

Medications are a godsend for medical issues. My son would live with unspeakable torment if it weren't for the finesse of his physicians and their prescriptions. But looking at 'ordinary' people, I am just wondering if the entire nation has become so depressed and in need of 'escape' that we must to be informed of the virtues of anti-depressants on an hourly basis.

We are all made of our own different fabric. Some people draw inner strength from external mechanisms and work well with parent support groups and organizations. Others draw inner strength and function much better avoiding the mixed energies of a group. I am one of the latter. When I have attempted to work with parent support groups, I found the issues, projects imposed, and extra duties took my focus away from my son. I don't know what or how parent groups are fairing now. Perhaps today they are more organized, more inclusive.

Many years ago, there appeared to be some sort of caste system going on. If your child was 'high functioning', you were in the *elite* group. If your child presented more of a depth to their difficulties, you were put on the back burner. I thought the caste system might have been a situation I had only imagined, but have heard the same sentiment echoed by some other older parents.

It seems, also, that the media pursues only the success stories of the very few people who came completely out of their autistic prisons. It gave false hope to those of us who tried so very hard. It was as though we hadn't tried hard enough, hadn't prayed fervently enough, hadn't loved enough. It was as though the severely autistic who couldn't 'open the door' and their families were hidden under the backyard shrubbery somewhere. Well guess what! We did try. We were fervent in our prayers and steadfast in our love. And we're still here.

Groups do not work for me, but I also know several mothers who take great comfort in the camaraderie and that's great. I thoroughly enjoy a one-on-one conversation with another parent who has walked the walk. It is with these mothers, especially we older ones, who can truly look back and laugh at where we've been. We old and seasoned moms naturally understand and bond with the young mothers. We are aware of the task ahead of them. We can truly appreciate and respect each other.

My friend Elaine sums up the bonding we mothers share eloquently. She states, "One of the greatest gifts our unique children with disabilities bring to our life as parents is this raw vulnerability they teach us. Because of this openness, we are able to forge these lasting and special relationships with other people living with disability in their everyday life. Only another 'special mother' understands the true joy of simply having a 'peaceful day'. They can truly celebrate with whole heat and soul the progress our child might achieve, such as touching a communication board in a meaningful way that day, as typical children receive music awards, graduations and weddings. A day that Shane enjoys without hurting himself or anyone else becomes as great of an accolade as someone else's child receiving a full scholarship. Only another parent in a similar position can grasp that and share. At the end of each long and tiring day, we are still gratefully that our 'special children' draw 'special people' to them, and hence to us. Shane has drawn and created a circle of love for me that will last a lifetime. I continue to celebrate him and his spirit even after he passes on. Can anyone ask for a better tribute or a stronger positive impact on the universe?" [Elaine - 2007]

Recently a mother and I were discussing remarks a friend had made to her about how 'fortunate' she was to be gifted with her daughter's autism. It brought to mind some of 'same old-same old' comments I, as well as other mothers, have heard too, too many times. Some of the classics are, "There will be an extra jewel in your crown when you get to heaven!", "You have certainly be blessed!", "You are a wonderful person" and so on. I think the comment that turns my stomach completely upside down is, "You are never given more than you can handle, dear!" Where do these people come from? You are at your wit's end. Your child lives in some far away, bizarre world and acts like you are a rock. In addition, your marriage has failed, the bills are piling up, you fear for the sanity and safety of your other children, and no one knows what abyss you've fallen in to. Yes, it is more than you can handle! You're falling apart, internally, and this idiot is telling you that you're wonderful and oh, by the way, you certainly CAN handle anything. Then they trot away to their complete, sane family. Or lunge into a dialogue about the major difficulties in their life, which may be as earth shattering as trying to determine which color of bathroom towels they should purchase to match the new tiling they've had installed. We older moms have shared laughter and giggles over some of the ridiculous 'compliments' we've received.

Real friends make you laugh. They may cry with you, but they don't cause the tears. Real friends make you realize there's still a real individual inside of you. They may not have autism in their life, but they bear scars from their own personal trials by fire. Support comes from a mutual understanding of and respect for where you both are in life's journey. Support can come from a neighbor just dropping off freshly baked cookies. Support can come in silence, without words.

Everyone should have a friend whose mere presence not only allows, but encourages one to 'center' and to be grounded to reality. Scheduling and self-imposed attitude changes in the fall of 2007 allowed me to reconnect with my old ally and confidant Glenda.   Allowing ourselves to return to home base occasionally reconnects us to who we truly are sans the perceived or validated stresses we face daily.

I am fortunate to have a few close friends. Miles also has his network of friends and comrades. Shane has no one, save for paid staff and family.   In the past, he became very attached to several of his direct care workers. When their time together ended, they always promised him that they would keep in touch as they left to go into other areas. They *promised* him they would 'visit real soon'. They never did.

I always hesitate to give a young parent 'hope'. I do not know what they may internally be hoping for. When Shane was younger, I hoped and prayed for a cure. It wasn't meant to be. The only 'hope' I would venture to offer is that young parents hope for a trusting and solid relationship with their child. With love, with caring, this is attainable. It is also wonderful.

Yes, some people will 'come out', leaving their autistic tendencies behind. There are still other 'high functioning' persons who will lead productive and independent lives. But please realize there are many Shane Boldts in the world. As each person with autism is unique to their own personality, likes and dislikes, I cannot say Shane Boldt will be somehow 'duplicated'. I am only stating that there are and there will be many individuals who will require enormous support and acceptance. The slight degree of progress he has made has been hard earned. We celebrate his 'little victories' but realize he will always be a captive slave to autism.

In lieu of hope, what I would freely offer is support. We are not in this boat alone. With the trials of caring for an autistic child, inner strengths are gained. When I think of caring, I'm not implying that a parent is actually performing the hands-on task of care giving. I find the verbs of caring and loving interchangeable. Although Shane spent much of his life away from me, I never stopped caring, or loving, or fighting for him.

I do know that I was terribly naïve as a young mother. I trusted advice from professionals simply because they were professionals, even though the advice didn't feel right, at gut level. I would have sought second and third opinions. Fighting for a loved one will toughen you up, if you have a tendency to be wishy-washy. And it will soften you up if you come on too strong. The system flows a lot more smoothly with honey than vinegar.

Ultimately, the parent holds responsibility for everything that happens to and for their child. It may be in the form of giving direct care or of supervising other persons to care for their person. Even when Shane was away from me, I was the one who was responsible for approving his programming, for signing on the appropriate dotted lines, and for constantly watching for signs of trouble. It's that ever-present second skin we wear.

As I cannot write of our experiences from Shane's viewpoint, neither can I speak for Miles. He has also chosen a very difficult path and I hope what he has learned thus far will aid him in his journey. He will always be Shane's co-guardian and will be called upon to sign papers, to validate programming and to watch from a distance. But I cannot emphasis enough that I would NOT want him to dedicate his entire life giving care to his brother. Already he has ventured, on his own, more support to me than I can ever recognize or repay. While it has appeared on many occasion that Shane has my soul, Miles surely has my heart.

I know many parents who are adamant in their attempts to provide siblings with outside supports and interests. They continually work diligently to give an equal percent of love, time and energy to all of their children. But when autism is involved, I feel a sibling will always feel that is their afflicted brother or sister who *really* gets most of their parent's time and efforts. It doesn't matter how hard you try or how many programs you enroll your sibling in. A parent may be enthusiastic when explaining how a sibling can go to camp, or grandmas or wherever and have fun away from the turmoil of the home. But the sibling probably feels the family member with autism is always on the front burner and getting the majority of the attention. Sometimes it is simply a matter of autism itself being so demanding.

If the child with autism is going to camp or has special meetings in the home, it's vice versa…the sibling may feel their brother/sister get special things they can't have. Some of these issues are normal sibling rivalry. Some of the issues are deeper and you really won't know how autism has impacted the sibling until they have grown into adulthood. It's a difficult juggling act raise children equally, but differently. It is balancing an illogical world with the logical world.

When Miles was small, I would try to read to him, attempt to spend time when he wanted. But more often than not, a younger Shane would run, shrieking, into the room, smearing himself or intentionally breaking/ tearing something for attention. Miles was short-changed in the attention department on more than one occasion. At other times, he would hide under the dining room table or in his room when Shane was out of control. How they managed to connect and create a bond is a wonder.

Growing up, it's hard to have your friends over when there's the chance your brother may run into the room, performing the same attention getting acts that he did as a toddler. It's embarrassing at best, and even worse when the sibling enters puberty and adolescence.

From the very day he was born, Miles was of great comfort to me. We spent all stolen moments together, going special places and having special times we could not have when Shane was around us. As an adult, Miles has a deep understanding of the complexity, and fragility of life. He has learned what is truly important in the soul's journey, and what is of little consequence. He still works direct care with his brother.

He knows what Shane is capable of accomplishing and pushes him to succeed more than I do. It is a strategy that works for them. Shane has an immense respect and adoration of his brother. There is a bond.

They can laugh, tease, and understand each other in a manner unavailable to anyone else connected to Shane. They can also 'argue' and disagree. When appropriate, Miles tells Shane he is acting like a jerk. Shane may throw back his favorite retaliatory remark, "You a bundt cake!". There is room to just be brothers. There are times when Shane is on the verge of a 'going out of control' mode when he will ask for "Baby Miles". Somehow Miles has become a respected safety net for him.

At the time of Shane's birth, the odds of having a child with autism were low. Today, I've heard the chances of a child being born with some form of autism are 1 in every 150 births. The increase of autism is prevalent in every *industrialized* country of the world.

I've often thought all of this madness may be a case of our living out the final chapters of Arthur C. Clarke's classic fiction novel, Childhood's End. Perhaps he was not only a gifted science fiction writer, but also a prophet. I do not make this statement lightly.

There have been numerous trends which claim to state what factors may cause autism. Currently some persons say it is directly linked to the immunization shots given to infants and small children. I knew we were in trouble prior to Shane receiving his shots and even then his pediatrician withheld some of the shots due to the difficult birth Shane had experienced. Childhood immunizations may be the etiology for some children, but I do not believe they are responsible for most of the increase in autism we are witnessing.

High school chemistry was definitely not one of my talents. I barely passed the course. Therefore, I do not claim to be an expert, or even a novice when it comes to the science of chemistry. However, I am entitled to an opinion after decades of observing Shane and other people with similar difficulties.

There are always allergies present, as well as food preferences. Shane is a cheese addict and we struggle to get other foods into his diet. Bribery works well. Eat your broccoli and you can have some pepper cheese. Other favorites are Colby cheese, Swiss cheese, string cheese, provolone and on, but he also likes buttermilk, beef sticks, and summer sausage. I refuse to have 'regular' milk in our home. I am aware of the controversy of casein and autism. For three decades every program he has been in has been unsuccessful with diet intervention. Fortunately he does accept and like other foods, inclusive of fish, potatoes, and other groups, which provide variety. That, of course, is contingent upon when he *chooses* to accept.

There are all sorts of way to sneak added nutrients into someone's diet. We always keep a two-gallon container of water in the refrigerator with cut fresh lemons inside. Cut apples, oranges and/or pears in water also make a rather tasty drink.

I believe the allergies are only a symptom, not the cause. I am one of a growing number of people who believe environmental issues have already effected (and continue to do so) in an extremely negative fashion.

Through the magic of television, I have heard and followed the theory [that] the actual number of autistic individuals has not actually increased. Rather, it is a matter of correctly diagnosing those persons who would have otherwise bore the diagnosis of being developmentally delayed. I disagree with the theory. From my experience in 'the field', I have watched the number of persons to appear to be truly autistic increase. When I started working with the population, most of the people I met appeared to be functioning within a varied range of mental retardation. Now I notice many children display the 'classic' outward mannerisms of autism, as opposed to being strictly mentally challenged.

The special education teachers and classroom aides I have had the pleasure of meeting tell me that the number of children displaying 'autistic tendencies' has increased dramatically.

While writing a college paper, I wrote an essay on what I felt was the etiology of autism. The computer my paper was stored in went belly-up and my only hard copy was lost when our basement flooded last year. But my thoughts have not changed and the more I read and view, the more I am convinced mankind and 'progress' are at the core of autism's etiology.

During the early and latter years of man's evolution, many thousands/millions of years passed before we realized the changes which we recognize today. It took time for migrating people to acclimate to their new surroundings. Adaptation did not come easily. So why would we possibly think the human body could adapt to the changes in the last one hundred years with ease? Did anyone really stop to contemplate the effects man made chemicals may actually have on the human body?

There are thousands of chemicals and chemical combinations abundant in our world today. They are abundant in every *industrialized* country in our world. Is the human body rebelling? Is it unable to absorb chemical substances and to pass it on to the needed organs? Are the chemicals themselves poisoning our systems to the point we cannot function as we were intended to do? The human body is a wondrous thing. It is also very fragile. To think we are mutating is a frightening thought. Yet we see the effects of modern technology and chemicals on other of our planet's life forms. It is a chilling theory.

Specifically, I am concerned with the effect petroleum based products may have had on our species.

Petroleum based products are used in, or in the manufacture of, almost every product we consume. These products are in certain medications, plastic, cosmetics, wax paper, recreational items, toys, many building materials, carpeting, paint, fertilizers, chewing gum, car batteries, non-cotton clothing. The list is much longer than I care to know about. But it gives us a picture of how much we depend on chemicals. Our foods are wrapped in plastic and our lives are wrapped in plastic. We eat, drink, breathe and breathe man-made chemicals daily. We even sleep with them. We bombard our bodies with petroleum-based products daily with little or no thought to the effect they might have on our systems or on the children yet to be born.

There's no way of reversing history to take an alternate route. In the world of technology, we have progressed with amazing speed and continue to do so. Progress in some areas has been of great can benefit to mankind. There have been tremendously beneficial advancements in the fields of medicine and science. I also believe progress in yet other areas has been detrimental to humanity and should have been seriously scrutinized prior to implementation to the masses. There might very well be unknown consequences and dues to be paid for our haste. I am not opposed to experimentation for the sake of progress. It is trial and error at the expense of living, breathing entities which I find questionable and appalling.

We live in an instant society. If it is convenient, we blindly accept it. We do not ask or ponder over alternative routes. If we stop now to scrutinize the issues that should have been investigated so many years ago, it won't matter. The dye has been cast. We have permanently altered the environment. We either adapt or we don't.

The bottom line is that the world is over populated and in our attempts to accommodate the masses, we've cut corners that should not have been sheared. I believe we've screwed ourselves royally. Personally, I think Mother Nature has had enough of our folly and I feel she'll be the one who nails us. Is the term (Mother Nature) inclusive of the galaxies and beyond areas which surround our planet Earth? We cannot forget the reports of the increased activity of meteors, meteorites and comets which pose a significant threat. If Shane would let me, I'd pull the covers over my head and sleep for the next five years.

It doesn't paint an attractive picture. So many factors are effecting our world today. We live with the effects of the current global warming and wars for profit. Governments that should be by the people and for the people now appear to ignore the people. Mortgage foreclosures abound. The number of homeless veterans and families is on the rise. Worldwide, there is genocide in third world countries, mass starvation in still other countries, and wide spread diseases. Our world through the centuries has become a haven for crime, corruption and pursuit of the almighty dollar. And the number of our children born with some form of autism increases. Mankind certainly isn't a species that learns from its mistakes.

And while I'm rambling, I may also add I feel the communication methods and devices of today leave little room for face-to-face human contact. It does not allow us to see the subtleties which offer insight to the true content of any given conversation. It is good that we have become a global community able to communicate longer distances, with more people in a shorter period of time. However, we are losing the fine art of warmth and personal contact. Will we forfeit the ability to understand and 'read' each other's intent? It is a tragic loss.

Considering all of the possibilities, we could choose to worry, stew and fight the hoard of perceived dragons. Or, we might just take the attitude of "O....pffffl!" We need to choose our battles wisely and quite frankly, some of them aren't worth the effort. It's a matter of perspective, which differs within each of us.

I don't know if I am cynical by nature or if it is due to life experiences. Getting older has its advantages. I can grump and complain about issues. Most of the time, people are condescending because I am aging. That's a fun thing that comes with the advancing years. If the Lord truly loveth a *cheerful* giver, then I have some major issues working.

With regards to autism, I would hope allopathic medicine would seek to couple with homeopathic resources to better serve our people. When Shane was young, rubbing a few drops of essential oil (tangerine) over his adrenal glands would calm him IF we could use it before he reached that point of no return. Even now, we've noted diffusing an essential oil blend (Citronella, Rosemary, Lemongrass, Lavender, Melaleuca and Myrtle) will ease his sinus distress. It is also an excellent blend if household molds are present. I purchase this blend from an established company and leave the expertise of correct proportioning to them.

Some other mothers I know use a variety of oils, usually by diffusion. Lavender and Sweet Orange are pleasant and relaxing. Blends of selected oils specifically created to calm are readily available. Allergies must be taken into consideration when using any homeopathic resource. Also, many essential oils, which are labeled 'pure', may only contain a few drops of the oil, to which filler is added. There are only two companies I purchase from because they are reputable and reliable.

There have also been periods in Shane's life when he has accepted Healing Touch, an energy technique. Although he isn't often receptive, it does have a calming and balancing effect. As with everything, his short attention span doesn't allow the practitioner time to accomplish what they'd like.

Shane doesn't readily accept body massage, but will allow bodywork to his legs and arms for short periods of time. Consistently, he is uneasy with massage in the vicinity of his upper three charkas. Reflexology is his favorite therapy although that, too, must be performed in very short sessions. There are therapies I feel would be beneficial, but it is his body and he knows what he can tolerate. That, in itself, must be respected.

As I age, I am more acutely aware that the day may come when I can no longer oversee Shane's care. I am also aware, from working in 'the field', that Shane may precede me in death. Many persons who have been exposed to long-term dosages of certain medications do have shorter life expectancies. The gradual but continual decrease in his neurological functions is of concern.

People have asked me why I chose to oversee Shane's care in a home setting at this stage of my life. The answer is quite clear and simple. I am determined to allow him to live with safety and security for at least a portion of his years as an adult. I know the son who exists inside his prison of autism. He deserves to have the sense of family belonging he has desperately craved, even if we can only provide that on a short-term basis. If we only have a few years of 'doing it Shane's way', then that will have to be enough. He is much slower, less intense in this stage of his life. Maturation and neurological decline have allowed him to slow down a little. He can now meet me half way as we struggle to support his needs. I chose to provide care for Shane at this time because I can.

Perhaps I also chose to be with Shane at this stage of my life because this may be our 'last stand' together.

The day may well come when I would choose to place Shane under the care of an agency again. It is my sincerest wish that he acclimates to any change in that direction.   I urge his direct care staff to work fervently on his self-help skills as his health permits, should he need to fall back on those attributes and successes. If such a day comes, it will be due to my retirement, failing health, or my demise. Until that day, I will continue to support my son and hope he continues to progress. Beyond that, I can offer no more. *We can only do what we can, while we can.* I have worked toward the goal of Shane's being able to remain in his familiar apartment. I would hope he could remain with safe, familiar staff.

Those of us with special needs children, no matter what their age, appear to be acutely aware for the need to provide for their future. There is no gauge or crystal ball that can tell us what plans to make, or when. I have attempted to cast a safety net for Shane so that he can stay in his apartment should I cross over first.

I have heard it echoed by so many mothers that they hope they can live one minute longer than their child so they can protect and provide for them until 'the end'.

I do not know what I would do should Shane no longer require my presence and support. Perhaps I would opt to experience yet another train trip to Arizona. I do know it would be pleasing to live long enough to see the day when I might, without regret, throw my computer out of the upstairs window. There is a nearby lake destined to receive my cell phone.

I am an avid admirer of Kahlil Gibran. Within _The Prophet_, he tells of our children not belonging to us and offers inspiration to let our children live their own lives. His literary works are absolutely beautiful. I wish he had written advice for those of us with children who are so fragile, so vulnerable, so misunderstood that they cannot walk their path alone.

Shane fills our lives to the point there is little, if any, room for anything else. Yet, in a Catch 22, he also drains us of our essence. He pulls us into a zone, which is somewhere between his world of autism and a world of our own making. He takes our energies with an intensity that would leaves us void. Long periods of time with Shane can leave a person drained, emotionally and physically. I wonder if he, too, feels exhausted in his exposure to us. Very, very often I wonder how he is, living within the core of an alien world.

My son has taught me many things. My favorite teacup isn't as important as finding out the reason he felt he to break it. People in our society talk too much and say very little. Too much energy is wasted on activities of little consequence or importance. You don't always have to explain yourself or your actions …to anyone. No one is more important or more valuable than any other person. You can't save the world; you can empathize with it, but you can't save it. Unconditional love reigns supreme. There is much truth in the adage, 'still waters run deep'. And of course, be true to yourself.

I have also learned that my son actually makes more sense than most of the world around us. Perhaps it is a matter of his being more evolved than those of us who only imagine we're on top of things.

Shane has also led us into areas of his world and I would thank him for his efforts. I hope we have been of comfort to him. I am extremely grateful for having this extremely honest and courageous man in my life.

Everyone on this planet has their own perception of reality and their very own personal story to tell. Life is a continually unfolding path that can take any of us just about anywhere.

This has been my perspective and our journey. Its just life. All we have to do is...get through it.

The author of this book may be contacted at:

P.O. Box 15314
Fort Wayne, IN   46815

.

www.ingramcontent.com/pod-product-compliance
Lightning Source LLC
Chambersburg PA
CBHW022112280326

41933CB00007B/352